D1369315

Introducing WinFX™

The Application Programming Interface for the Next Generation of Microsoft Windows Code Name "Longhorn"

Brent Rector

PUBLISHED BY
Microsoft Press
A Division of Microsoft Corporation
One Microsoft Way
Redmond, Washington 98052-6399

Library of Congress Cataloging-in-Publication Data pending.

Rector, Brent
    Introducing WinFX The Application Programming Interface for the Next Generation of Microsoft
        Windows Code Name "Longhorn" / Brent Rector.
            p. cm.

    Includes index.

    ISBN 0-7356-2085-7

Printed and bound in the United States of America.

1 2 3 4 5 6 7 8 9   QWT   8 7 6 5 4 3

Distributed in Canada by H.B. Fenn and Company Ltd.

A CIP catalogue record for this book is available from the British Library.

Microsoft Press books are available through booksellers and distributors worldwide. For further information about international editions, contact your local Microsoft Corporation office or contact Microsoft Press International directly at fax (425) 936-7329. Visit our Web site at www.microsoft.com/mspress. Send comments to *mspinput@microsoft.com*.

Acquisitions Editor: Robin Van Steenburgh
Project Editor: Kathleen Atkins
Copy Editors: Roger LeBlanc and Jennifer Harris

Body Part No. X10-25659

As always, I dedicate this book to Lisa, Carly, and Sean. I've finally convinced Lisa that one really does write a book by staring at the screen for days, occasionally poking a key on the keyboard. She has this funny thing about deadlines and typing in text. Carly's become dangerous now that she can write and understand code. But she likes my "Here thar be Dragons" comments in nasty pieces of code. My budding author, Sean, provides editorial comments that enliven my days. Thanks to you all for putting up with my mental, if not physical, time away while focused on this book.

Table of Contents

Acknowledgments

Without the support of the numerous people, this book wouldn't exist today. While everyone I mention has provided me invaluable help in one way or another and has made the book far better than it otherwise would have been, any remaining errors are entirely my fault.

First, I must thank Jim Allchin. He had the original idea for the book and that ultimately resulted in my ~~suffering~~, umm, creating this work. Seriously, though, Longhorn is such a fantastic new technology, and the experience of working with it and talking to those creating it was such great fun and so highly educational that it only occasionally seemed a Sisyphean task.

I'd also like to thank Brad Abrams and Darryn Dieken. Without their amazing support, there would be no book. Microsoft is such a large company and so many people are contributing to Longhorn that I was continually asking Brad and Darryn for guidance through the Minoan labyrinth that is Microsoft.

Nick Kramer deserves extraordinary mention and kudos. I can't thank him enough, so I'll simply say, "Thanks, Nick." Bill, you should give Nick a big raise.[1] Pablo Fernicola, Sean Grimaldi, Jeff Kirkham, and Yasser Shohoud also went out of their way to help.

Numerous other people helped me so many times, I've lost track. Those who come to mind are, in no particular order, Chris Anderson, Kevin Gjerstad, Vivek Dalvi, Mark Alcazar, Alex Hopmann, Peggi Goodwin, Mike Deem, Warren Barkley, Allen Marshall, Lisa Osse, Matt Rhoten, Ravi Soin, and David Switzer.

I must, of course, mention my Microsoft Press ~~torturers~~ editors, Robin Van Steenburgh and Kathleen Atkins. When I'd hit a roadblock, Robin would fix it. When ~~I would~~ I'd leave out a contraction, Kathleen would make me put it back in. She was assisted in her efforts by Roger LeBlanc and Jennifer Harris. Without their efforts, this bok wuld be mulch harder to reed. ☺

---

1. Yeah right. Like I actually know Bill. I have, though, seen him from the back of every single Professional Developers Conference!

Introduction

As a software developer of many, many years, I've written programs for numerous platforms and operating systems, all of which had their advantages and disadvantages. Generally, most platforms and operating systems were similar to their predecessors with incremental improvements.

To date, Microsoft Windows itself has evolved this way. Initially, writing a Windows application meant programming to the Microsoft Win32 API.[1] Microsoft designed the Win32 API as a flat, procedural API callable by C programs. At one time, Charles Petzold's book *Programming Windows*, which introduced this API, was required reading for any Windows application developer.

The nice thing about the Win32 API is that it lets you do pretty much anything you want.[2] You get first crack at all Windows messages and can respond to the events that they signal in any appropriate (or inappropriate) way. You can modify memory—your own process's memory or even another process's memory—however you want, security permitting. You can draw a window any way you like. You job is *simply* to get the correct bits to the screen in the correct places at the proper times.

The design of Windows itself is actually quite object-oriented. You manipulate window *objects*, use graphical *pens*, and so forth. However, you perform these operations by calling the correct APIs (out of the thousands available) in the proper order and passing the proper data types, mostly without compiler help when you get it wrong.

When Microsoft first released Windows and for a number of years after, software developers typically wrote monolithic, isolated applications. Developers had no components from which to compose applications and no mechanism that supported composition, and applications did not attempt to communicate with other applications on the same system, let alone with an application on a different computer.

In 1993, Microsoft introduced the Component Object Model (COM). Microsoft designed COM as an attempt to solve the following two problems. COM introduced a binary standard so that components, produced by different source language compilers, could interoperate using immutable interface

---

1. Actually, it was the Win16 API at one time, but they're conceptually the same.
2. The less nice thing is that you pretty much *must* do everything you want.

definitions. The Distributed COM (DCOM) network protocol allowed these components to interact across process and machine boundaries.

Many of the Windows APIs that Microsoft introduced after 1993 are COM-based APIs. Two examples are the DirectX and Shell extensions APIs. Today, Windows has over 10,000 APIs designed by many different developers on many different teams with different goals. As a result, Windows exposes some of the APIs as flat, C-language entry points in a dynamic-link library (DLL). It exposes other APIs as a set of complex, interacting COM interfaces. There are other APIs that you access using other technologies.

In practice, you, the developer, want an operating system to shield you from most of this complexity most of the time. Therefore, many different teams, within Microsoft and without, developed various framework libraries to simplify application development. Some popular framework libraries are the Microsoft Foundation Classes (MFC), the Microsoft ActiveX Template Library (ATL), Microsoft Visual Basic's library, Borland's Object Windows Library (OWL), and no doubt many others.

MFC, for example, attempts to wrap the various idiosyncrasies of the Win32 API with a consistent and object-oriented set of C++ classes. When your programming language of choice is C++ and the MFC libraries directly support what you want to do, your job is easy. However, when you want something slightly outside the mainstream, you are mostly on your own again and, in fact, in worse shape than before because now you have to figure out how to use the Win32 APIs, plus make your work interoperate with the existing MFC classes.

ATL lets you write extremely efficient COM objects, and to a lesser extent Windows applications, using obscure and, to many developers, poorly understood C++ template-based classes. It's not a far stretch to say that you could easily end up with highly efficient objects that no one could understand.

Microsoft's Visual Basic team took a different approach. They wrapped access to the Win32 API in an easy to learn and use language and library, but at the expense of removing functionality and options. Visual Basic makes it extremely simple to produce components for applications and the applications that use such components. However, Visual Basic doesn't allow you complete access to everything the Win32 API offers. Sometimes the Visual Basic developer simply cannot accomplish a task because of restrictions imposed by the chosen development environment.

In the early to mid-1990s, the World Wide Web took off. Computers started to become more and more connected. Initially, a Web browser simply rendered static HTML, and browsing the Web was a lot like looking at a magazine page.

When Microsoft released Internet Explorer 4 in 1997, other possibilities arose. Developers could create HTML files containing script plus markup.

Objects in the HTML object model gained behaviors, and you could write script that responded to events and provided customized behavior. HTML pages could now react to user events on the client and respond far more quickly than prior Web-based applications that required a roundtrip to the server for each screen update.

One big advantage of Web applications was that you could easily deploy the application by simply copying over a set of files to a server. The next time a client browsed to the application, she interacted with the latest version.

Another big advantage of Web applications was the built-in support for rich media integration. Flow-based page layout and support for multiple fonts, graphics, and multimedia content is far easier to provide via a Web application than it currently is via a Win32 application, regardless of the framework you use.

Overall, however, it's still difficult to write Web applications today because programming language and library support for such applications is limited. Debugging Web applications is often a nightmare. In many ways, the client user experience still isn't as rich as that provided by client applications based on the Win32 API because of the limited set of controls available to Web applications.

By the late 1990s, a Windows developer often had to specialize. You were a Win32 API programmer and could write any kind of client application slowly. Alternatively, you were a Visual Basic developer and could write relatively rich, form-based user interface (UI) applications quickly but couldn't write certain other types of applications at all. An MFC developer somewhat straddled these two extremes, although in practice, you needed to be a proficient C++ developer who was familiar with the Win32 API to be a good MFC developer. ATL and COM-object developers were often the plumbers of a system and provided components for these other developers to reuse.

In 2000, Microsoft introduced .NET. The definition of what exactly .NET *is* differs depending on whom you ask. In my opinion, .NET is a modern software development platform for producing, more rapidly than one could previously, correct and secure Windows applications that use the latest technologies, such as XML, and Web services, while still allowing access to your heritage code.

.NET in general, and managed code in particular, provides a number of benefits to the software developer:

- An object-oriented, language-agnostic, type-safe object model.

- Reduced conflicts between different versions of components.

- Reduced number of bugs and security holes due to common programming mistakes. For example, there are no more buffer overruns and no more memory management errors.

- A single framework and set of libraries that all developers can use. The .NET Framework class libraries encapsulate the most commonly used Win32 APIs plus numerous additional APIs provided by many SDKs in a unified package.

- Higher abstractions than were previously available.

In some ways, .NET is simply a new object-oriented, language-agnostic framework that encapsulates many aspects of the Win32 APIs. Personally, I prefer to think of .NET as a state-of-the-art replacement for the Win32 APIs—incomplete as yet, but becoming more complete over time.

For example, .NET version 1.0 provides object-oriented, form-based client application development classes. You could think of these as simply wrappers over the basic Win32 windowing APIs. However, .NET also provides ASP.NET classes that encapsulate Web application development and HTML plus behavior generation. These classes in effect extend the Windows API and aren't really a wrapper for anything in the Win32 APIs. .NET's rich support for Web services and XML in general are two more examples of new functionality provided with .NET rather than simple wrappers around existing Win32 functionality.

What This Book Is About

This book focuses on the Microsoft Longhorn features for the developer. From a developer's point of view, Longhorn provides new functionality we can broadly categorize in five areas:

Longhorn Application Model

Longhorn defines applications in new, more powerful ways.

- Longhorn APIs are managed classes that handle much of the programming housekeeping and reduce the workload of the developer. All third-party developer compilers and tools that support the .NET Common Language Runtime (CLR) automatically support the new Longhorn APIs.

- The Longhorn application model supports both traditional form-based and new page-based navigation applications. Application page-based navigation support is provided by the operating system.

- A new Longhorn security and privacy model, which is the result of a combination of managed APIs and digital identity, provides application security from the beginning of the development process. Longhorn applications and components are trusted because of their use of managed code.

- The Longhorn APIs represent the best development concepts from a variety of contemporary technologies. In many ways, the developer is no longer constrained by design decisions made more than a decade ago.

- Automatic application state management and retention for easier application development.

- ClickOnce deployment technology supports sophisticated deployment features such as installation in Program Files, versioning, Side-By-Side installation, and Drizzle Download.

- Inductive UIs lead users through a task.

- Accessibility and automation features are built into the platform. Your applications automatically gain such support.

Trustworthy Computing and Security

Longhorn bases an application's security on the common language runtime code access security (CAS) model but with significant extensions.

- Longhorn recognizes that some applications are fully trusted and others have only partial trust. Applications that fully participate in the Longhorn security model will have full access to Longhorn's features. Applications that only partially participate in the model will have some benefits, albeit with restrictions.

- Longhorn provides an ultrasecure, managed-code, runtime environment, called the Secure Execution Environment (SEE), that protects the user from "bad" application behavior.

- The Trust Manager provides a scoring system for Longhorn applications that determines a suggested level of trust that users could grant to the application.

- Longhorn provides a security Trust Center that allows a user to manage hot fixes and access Windows updates. In addition, a Security Advisor informs the user of security risks and violations.

- Digital Rights Management is a part of managed code, giving strong protection for intellectual property. This allows secure storage and transmission of previously vulnerable intellectual property in the Longhorn environment.

- Longhorn uniquely identifies users and computers using digital signatures. When combined with a signing authority for verification, Longhorn can securely and reliably identify individual users in computing scenarios.

Rich Storage and Data Access

Longhorn provides significantly improved application data storage and access via a new file system.

- Windows Future Storage (WinFS) is the new Windows file system based on structured query language (SQL) technology.

- The new ADO.NET provides improved data access.

- Common schemas for everyday information, such as contacts, organizations, addresses, and much more, allow shared information access by applications, the operating system, and the shell. In fact, the new shell user interface is one of the heaviest users of the new storage system.

- An application can attach additional metadata to objects in the file system, which allows faster search and retrieval of file objects than is possible with a traditional file system.

- Changes in objects in the Longhorn environment are automatically propagated to other instances of those objects using dynamic data binding.

- WinFS allows easier propagation of data across clients and servers using data synchronization and replication, removing complexity for the developer.

Communication and Collaboration

Longhorn applications now have a rich variety of communication and collaboration features.

- Features such as sessions and channels provide rich collaboration services to participants.

- Communication and collaboration features can securely operate through firewalls and Network Address Translation (NAT), allowing traversal of corporate boundaries.

- Standardized communication based on Web services allows legacy and new applications to participate in collaboration.

- Server-based/peer-based communications features can operate over centralized infrastructure or directly to user clients.

- Virtual presence support allows users to collaborate with others through instant messaging–like features (common notification, invite, and so on).

- Integrated security is an integral part of these capabilities.

- Shell Extensibility support, such as collaborative verbs (use of a default chat client, and so on), can be identified to make use of familiar tools in Longhorn's real-time communication.

- Common controls such as the new People Picker control provide high-level application support for communication applications.

Rich Presentation and Media

Developers can more easily produce applications providing rich user interfaces using the presentation and media services available in Longhorn.

- Longhorn provides the developer with rich graphics classes that provide animation, effects, and visually exciting images that exploit hardware acceleration.

- Powerful declarative and dynamic vector graphics allow flexible presentation and scaling for high-resolution output devices while saving resources because graphics are generated from a descriptive language.

- Easily applied animations improve usability and continuity of the UI.

- Graphics support uses hardware accelerated DirectX/3D video cards to create a more immersive and fluid environment.

- Your application can seamlessly integrate all forms of user interface—images, video, audio, vector graphics, controls, text, and so on.

- A new layout model allows for rich text and media display because of a framework that automatically adjusts pagination, position, and so on to the screen size.

- New text services such as the inclusion of subpixel rendering (ClearType) allow for a visually engaging GUI on any PC with a 3D accelerator independent of possible screen resolutions.

- You can merge disparate pieces of data into containers, which can be moved around the UI.

- Conditional transformations of data based on type, value, or other rules gives the developer tools to create a more facile UI.

- An extensive multimedia platform allows a glitch-free playback of audio and video; distributed A/V experiences between PCs and consumer electronics devices; highest quality audio and video codecs; high performance for real-time, high-definition content capture and editing; rich CD, DVD, and television metadata services.

What You'll Find in This Book

Each of these topics can easily fill a book on its own. Therefore, I'm not going to describe all the various APIs in Longhorn. I'm also not going to dive into a detailed description of each technology. This is *not* an API or reference book. I'm sure it won't be long until you can find many slightly edited and regurgitated copies of the documentation available in bookstores.

What I am going to do is show you how to get started developing for Longhorn. At a minimum, you really should read Chapters 1 and 2 because they cover the absolute basics you need to know to develop applications for the Longhorn platform.

In Chapter 1, I discuss the new application model. Do not pass Go. Do not collect $200. You really need to read Chapter 1 or you'll get a Go To Jail card in the mail. I also introduce you to a new markup/programming language in Chapter 1. Whether you're a VB.NET developer, a C# developer, or one of the mythical COBOL.NET developers, you'll need to learn this new markup/programming language. Read Chapter 1. I'm not kidding. In fact, go do it now and come back. I'll wait....

Okay, now that you've read Chapter 1 and are excited to build your own applications, you probably should read Chapter 2. In it, I show you how to compile, deploy, and run a Longhorn application. So Chapter 2 is also important, but there's no need to rush off to it. It's a very patient chapter and will wait for you to finish this introduction.

The remaining chapters introduce the various technologies I've alluded to in this introduction. Chapter 3 is a fantastic introduction to creating user interfaces using the new markup language and gives you a flavor of its power. Chapter 4 introduces the new file system APIs and will likely cause you to abandon the Win32 file system APIs.

In Chapter 5, I show you how to use data binding to move data from practically any .NET object to your user interface and back again without writing any procedural code. I show you how to create powerful, secure, reliable communication applications in Chapter 6. And finally, the last chapter discusses some guidelines for creating modern, connected mobile applications.

Thanks for hanging out until the end of this long introduction. Now it's time for you to read Chapter 2. (You did go read Chapter 1 earlier, didn't you?) Have fun with Longhorn. I certainly have!

1

The Longhorn Application Model

Why do we need a new application model? One major reason is to bridge the gap between developing an application for Microsoft Windows and developing an application for the Web.

Today when you write a Windows application, you can take advantage of Windows features. Your application can provide a rich, responsive user interface. You can install the application on the client computer, which allows the application to run offline, without a network connection. Windows applications can take advantage of the hardware capabilities of the client computer.

However, traditional Windows applications also have a number of drawbacks. You typically must install a Windows application. This makes the application and any updates hard to deploy. Windows applications don't run in the browser. Therefore, familiar Web UI paradigms such as page-oriented applications, navigation directly from one page to another, page history, and more aren't available to your application unless you create them from scratch. Windows applications also don't support text very well, especially when you try to mix text and graphics on the same page. Creating a Windows application that automatically flows text around graphics and that responds to user-initiated changes in the window size and user preferences for fonts and readability is a huge amount of work.

Web applications have their own distinct strengths as well. When you browse to a Web page, the browser downloads only that page and the components the page requires. When you navigate to a new page, the browser then downloads the new page's requirements. In other words, the browser progressively downloads the application as needed.

Deployment of a Web application is trivial. What deployment? You place the necessary application components on a server, and the browser downloads them as needed. There's no deployment per se.

Creating the UI for a Web application is also quite easy. You declare your intentions using markup. For example, suppose I want a table in a specific position. I want an image to follow the table. I want some text to flow around the image. Mixing text, graphics, and media (sound and video) in a Web application is straightforward.

Of course, Web applications also have their bad points. You can't install a Web application on the desktop system; therefore, the application cannot run offline. You must always have a connection to the server. Certain application operations require roundtrips to the server, and that lessens performance. A Web application selection of controls is quite primitive in comparison to the available Windows controls. A Web application therefore typically has poor interactivity. It's also hard to develop an attractive UI for a Web application because you must express any non-trivial layout using tables.

Currently, developers designing new applications need to make an initial, huge, irreversible decision: should the application be a Web-style application or a classic Microsoft Win32 application? Completely separate programming models (and skills!) are needed depending on which application model you choose.

Longhorn allows you to develop applications using the best of both worlds. The Longhorn application model takes the best features of Web applications and the best features of Windows applications and combines them in a single unified programming model based on managed code.

A second major reason for developing a new application model is to provide a single programming model that can create the wide variety of "applications" in use today. Look at one of your favorite Web sites, such as CNN or MSNBC. Is the Web site a traditional application? Is it a document? Is it a multimedia presentation? In many cases, the answer is yes to all three questions.

When a Web site includes UI elements such as list boxes, edit controls, and radio buttons, it looks like an application presenting a UI. However, when it displays images and text flowing around the images, the Web site is similar to a document. When it presents Flash content, graphics, audio, video, and animation, the Web site seems to be a multimedia presentation.

Of course, such rich Web sites are difficult to develop. You need to patch together an HTML markup–based description of the page, with Microsoft ActiveX controls for a rich UI, with embedded Flash animations, and possibly using Portable Document Format (PDF) for document support. All these technologies use a different architecture, provide different performance characteristics, and require different programming models and tools.

This typically means that you must hire multiple developers with different skill sets to develop each portion of the application. The developers must then merge the different models into a single working application. Developing the application is hard enough. Debugging it is often a nightmare.

Longhorn provides a unified architecture that supports these three tiers—documents, applications, and media. Do you want to create your UI declaratively using markup? Go for it. Do you need to use rich Windows controls? Then do so! Do you want to write event handlers in a strongly typed, managed language? You can do that as well. Do you want to mix text, graphics, and video in a document with intelligent layout and presentation according to the user's preferences and optimized for best viewing and reading on the client system? Guess what? You get that too.

The Longhorn application model makes it possible to write an application using a single programming model that supports application-style UI functionality, document-style presentation of text and graphics, and integration of various media. In addition, you can create the UI using markup like a Web application. You also get the deployment (or lack of deployment) ease of a Web application. However, you still have the performance and ability to install the application for offline use like a Windows application. Your application can run as a stand-alone application or hosted in a Web browser by simply recompiling one source code base. In either case, your application can be form-based, like many traditional Windows applications, or page-based, like Web applications.

Features of the Longhorn Application Model

The Longhorn application model defines what an application is:

- Its entry points
- Its flow of control—how to navigate from one page to another
- Its shared state and resources
- Application-wide events
- Its isolation from other applications

The Longhorn application model defines how to deploy and maintain an application:

- Deployment as single or multiple files
- Update, rollback, and administration

The Longhorn application model defines the user's experience with the application:

- Zero-impact installation
- Stand-alone (Windows-style) or integrated in browser
- Runs online or offline
- Navigation model

Longhorn Web Applications

The Longhorn application model allows you to write a rich application similarly to the way you write today's Web applications. This provides an easy migration path for Web developers, as the code they write is similar to the code for dynamic HTML (DHTML) Web pages. They can (shudder) place markup and script in same file. They can deploy the files for the application to a Web server. The application pages run in the Web browser.

However, the object model for a Longhorn Web-style application is much simpler and far more powerful than DHTML. The application code can use the complete Longhorn presentation layer. Therefore, a Longhorn Web application can use rich client controls, support multimedia and graphics on the page, handle events locally—basically everything a normal client application might do. In fact, a Longhorn Web application isn't much different from a Longhorn desktop application other than that the files live on a server; a browser typically, but not necessarily, hosts the UI; and the application runs with restricted permissions because the user hasn't installed it on the client system.

Longhorn Desktop Applications

The Longhorn application model also defines how to write desktop applications. A *Longhorn desktop application* is an application that the user has installed locally. Such applications can run online or offline. Such applications can register with the shell, place icons on the desktop, add shortcuts to the Start menu, and more.

A desktop application can also run in the browser window or in a stand-alone window. In fact, a desktop application can support many features traditionally associated with a Web application, including the following:

- Explicitly define external entry points—that is, can start on any page
- Share state across pages
- Handle various events, including page navigation events

- Control application flow
- Add/remove entries from a page history/travel navigation log
- Launch application windows

Building a Longhorn Application

To build a Longhorn application, you define the object model for your application. You can define the model programmatically by writing code or declaratively by writing markup in a language called the Extensible Application Markup Language (XAML). You compile your code and/or markup into one or more .NET assemblies, an application manifest file, and a deployment manifest file.

Optionally, you can package your application into a new file format, called a *container*. The application files in a container can be compressed, encrypted, and digitally signed.

I discuss building a Longhorn application in detail in Chapter 2, but for now the main idea is that building a Longhorn application gives you the application's code, an application manifest that describes all the components that the application uses, and a deployment manifest that tells the system how to install and maintain the application.

Deploying a Longhorn Application

The Longhorn application model provides for easy, cost-effective deployment of your application. In the simplest case, you simply copy the application files to a server. Similarly, installing your application is straightforward and non-impactful.

One option is not to install the application at all. The user can browse to the application manifest on a server and run it. Longhorn incrementally downloads your application and executes it. You get no confirmation demands, no reboot requirements, and no DLL hell. In fact, you do not even need Administrator rights to install or run the application.

Alternatively, the user can browse to the application's deployment manifest on the server and run it. Longhorn incrementally downloads your application, installs it, and executes it. By default, all Longhorn applications run in a limited permission environment called the Secure Execution Environment (SEE).

Applications running in the SEE receive a restricted permission set that is roughly equivalent to the permissions granted to today's applications associated with the Internet zone. An application that requires additional permissions than Longhorn provides by default must request those additional permissions in its application manifest.

The first time the user runs such an application, the Longhorn Trust Manager will evaluate the elevated permission request, notify the user of a suggested risk level associated with granting the application's permission request, and provide a suggested response for that risk level. When the user permits the Trust Manager to grant the application its requested permissions, the Trust Manager records this information. Subsequent executions of the installed application proceed without the security warning.

Today, when you install an application locally, it receives the FullTrust permission set simply because it loads from the LocalComputer zone. Code Access Security (CAS) works differently for Longhorn applications. A local (or installed) application runs under the security policy of the site from which the user downloaded it instead of automatically receiving FullTrust simply because it is installed locally.

When loading an application, its components, and its resources, Longhorn provides evidence to the common language runtime (CLR) security system such as

- Internet zone and site of origin (from the Uniform Resource Identifier [URI])

- Publisher and module name (from the deployment manifest)

CAS then provides security policy–based enforcement over access privileges based on the application's evidence.

The deployment manifest for an application can specify the update interval that Longhorn should use when checking for a new version of the application. When Longhorn detects that a new version is available, it downloads and installs the new version in the background. The next time the user runs the application, she receives the new version.

When installing an application, Longhorn preserves the previous version, if any. Should you need to, you can painlessly roll back to the previous version or even completely uninstall the application using Add/Remove Programs. IT departments can push the installation of an application to a client system for a hands-free deployment.

You specify how to deploy the application when you compile the project, and you can change the deployment scenario by recompiling, typically with few or no changes to your source code.

A developer's program initially interacts with much of Longhorn's application support via an instance of the *MSAvalon.Windows.Application* class, so let's look at that class.

The *Application* Class

A Longhorn program always contains a single instance of an application object. This object derives directly or indirectly from the *MSAvalon.Windows.Application* class and performs the following functions:

■ Provides an entry point, encapsulation, and scope for the application

■ Allows an application to share code and state across the pages that make up the application

■ Provides application-level events

■ Maintains a collection of the application's windows

■ Provides a security model

■ Defines any resources that the application uses

The *MSAvalon.Windows.Application* class provides basic application support to an application. You typically use it when your application needs low overhead and does not use page navigation features. However, most Longhorn platform applications use the closely related *MSAvalon.Windows.Navigation-Application* class, which inherits from *MSAvalon.Windows.Application* and adds support for navigation. I'll discuss the *NavigationApplication* class in detail in the following section. You will typically define a class that inherits the appropriate base class, overrides base class methods as necessary, and then registers for events to provide custom startup or shutdown procedures.

The SimpleApplication1.cs source file listing, shown here, demonstrates using the *Application* object. The *EntryClass.Main* method sets the threading state to ApartmentState.STA,[1] creates my specialized application object, *MyApp*, and calls its *Run* method to launch the application. The *MyApp* class overrides the *OnStartingUp* method, which receives control when the application is starting up. When the system invokes the *OnStartingUp* method, I call a helper method that creates the application's main window, adds some text to the window, and displays the window

SimpleApplication1.cs

```
using System;
using MSAvalon.Windows;
using MSAvalon.Windows.Controls;
using MSAvalon.Windows.Media;
```

---

1. Technically, you only need to set the threading state in code-only applications. Applications that use XAML don't need their threading state initialized.

```
namespace IntroLonghorn {
  public class MyApp : MSAvalon.Windows.Application {
    MSAvalon.Windows.Controls.SimpleText txtElement;
    MSAvalon.Windows.Window              mainWindow;

    protected override void OnStartingUp (StartingUpCancelEventArgs e) {
      base.OnStartingUp (e);
      CreateAndShowMainWindow ();
    }

    private void CreateAndShowMainWindow () {
      // Create the application's main window
      mainWindow = new MSAvalon.Windows.Window ();

      // Add a dark red, 14 point, "Hello World!" text element
      txtElement = new MSAvalon.Windows.Controls.SimpleText ();
      txtElement.Text = "Hello World!";
      txtElement.Foreground = new
        MSAvalon.Windows.Media.SolidColorBrush (Colors.DarkRed);
      txtElement.FontSize = new FontSize (14,
                                          FontSizeType.Point);
      mainWindow.Children.Add (txtElement);
      mainWindow.Show ();
    }
  }

  internal sealed class EntryClass {
    [System.STAThread]
    private static void Main () {
      MyApp app = new MyApp ();
      Thread.CurrentThread.ApartmentState = System.Threading.ApartmentState.STA;
      app.Run ();
    }
  }
}
```

I used the following command line to compile the SimpleApplication1.cs source code into an executable application. You might need to adjust the paths to the referenced assemblies.

```
csc /r:C:\WINDOWS\Microsoft.NET\Windows\v6.0.4030\PresentationCore.dll
    /r:C:\WINDOWS\Microsoft.NET\Windows\v6.0.4030\PresentationFramework.dll
    /r:C:\WINDOWS\Microsoft.NET\Windows\v6.0.4030\WindowsBase.dll
    SimpleApplication1.cs
```

The *Application* class contains a number of other useful properties, methods, and events. For example, your application class can override the *OnShuttingDown* virtual method to provide custom shutdown behavior. The application class also provides the *StartingUp* and *ShuttingDown* events so that other classes can register for startup and shutdown notifications. The

Shutdown method allows you to initiate the shutdown of the application programmatically.

You might want to reference your application object from multiple places in your source code. Therefore, the *Application* class provides the *Current* static property that returns a reference to your application object. The following code fragment uses the *Current* property to locate the application object and register for a shutdown event notification:

```
MyApp app = (MyApp) MSAvalon.Windows.Application.Current;
  app.ShuttingDown += new
      Application.ShuttingDownEventHandler (ShutDownHandler);
  ⋮
private static void
 ShutDownHandler (object sender, MSAvalon.Windows.ShuttingDownEventArgs e) {
  ⋮
}
```

The *NavigationApplication* Class

When you want navigation support for your application, you'll typically use the *MSAvalon.Windows.Navigation.NavigationApplication* class, which extends the *MSAvalon.Windows.Application* class. Although you can build a navigation-based application without using the *NavigationApplication* class, using the class provides the following additional capabilities to your application:

- Simplifies writing navigation-based applications; not usually necessary to subclass the class

- Determines when a connection is available

- Provides navigation events—such as *Navigating*, *NavigationProcess*, *Navigated*, *NavigationError*, *LoadCompleted*, and *Stopped*—which it fires when the appropriate event occurs in any of the application's windows

- Shares state across pages

- Provides a container for property values shared across pages

- Implements a policy that opens an initial window by default

Externally, a navigation application's user can navigate only to well-defined entry points of the application. Internally, however, the developer controls navigation by hooking events. You can determine when a window or frame attempts to navigate to a new page and when the navigation is complete. You can cancel or redirect any navigation. You can find out the identity of the target page. You can handle navigation errors.

The familiar navigation model makes an application easy to use. A navigation application provides behavior similar to the Web. Your application can use hyperlinks, provide Forward and Back buttons, display a Favorites list, and maintain a page History. The Longhorn *NavigationApplication* class and related classes provide all the support for such features.

A navigation application works whether online or offline, and it works the same whether a browser hosts the application or the application runs as a stand-alone. In addition, you have complete control over this Weblike behavior. You can customize the user experience as required. You can insert, remove, and modify Travelog entries to control where the Forward and Back operations go. You can define which pages (entry points) are logged in the History.

A navigation application typically creates one or more instances of the *MSAvalon.Windows.Navigation.NavigationWindow* class. The Simple-Application2.cs listing, shown here, demonstrates a use of these classes. This listing is the same as SimpleApplication1.cs except that it uses the *Navigation-Application* and *NavigationWindow* classes.

SimpleApplication2.cs

```
using System;
using MSAvalon.Windows;
using MSAvalon.Windows.Controls;
using MSAvalon.Windows.Media;
using MSAvalon.Windows.Navigation;

namespace IntroLonghorn {
  public class MyApp : MSAvalon.Windows.Navigation.NavigationApplication {

    protected override void OnStartingUp (StartingUpCancelEventArgs e) {
      base.OnStartingUp (e);
      CreateAndShowMainWindow ();
    }

    private void CreateAndShowMainWindow () {

      // Create the application's main window
      mainWindow = new MSAvalon.Windows.Navigation.NavigationWindow ();

      // Fill window with appropriate controls
      :
      // Show the window
      mainWindow.Show ();
    }
  }

  internal sealed class EntryClass {
    [System.STAThread]
```

```
private static void Main () {
Thread.CurrentThread.ApartmentState = System.Threading.ApartmentState.STA;
  MyApp app = new MyApp ();
  app.Run ();
}
  }
}
```

The code you've seen up to now is just another variation on traditional programming models. The only new aspect is the actual classes I've used. Most of the time, however, you won't actually write much of this code. Let's take a slight detour and learn about a new programming language that allows you to write this same code in a much more compact and—to me, at least—more understandable manner.

Extensible Application Markup Language (XAML)

In many applications, much of the code you write pertains to creating and updating the UI of the application. In fact, in the previous examples, there was no code other than that required to create the UI. In the last few years, many developers have learned to write, and even to prefer to define, an application's UI by using one of a number of available markup languages. The Longhorn platform defines a new markup language named the Extensible Application Markup Language (XAML; pronounced "Zamel," which rhymes with "camel").

Using a markup language to define a UI has a number of advantages over using a procedural programming language. These advantages include the following:

- More apparent control hierarchies

- More apparent property inheritance

- Easier processing and interpretation of markup language by tools

- Potential separation of UI and procedural code

I like XAML, and I prefer to use it to define my UIs rather than using the procedural-type coding I've shown you so far in this chapter. However, don't think that you'll be able to do everything you'll need to by using nothing but XAML.

Consider this statement from the documentation: "Documents can often be written entirely in XAML and displayed in the browser." I hastily point out that this sentence uses the word *documents*, not *applications*, and it qualifies the statement with the term *often*. When you're writing a document that displays static content, you can create it in pure XAML. You can even write a document that uses data binding to display and update content from a data source by using nothing but XAML. You can define animations and mouse-over effects by using nothing but XAML. You can do a heck of a lot using nothing but XAML. (In fact, I try to do as much as possible in XAML and as little as possible in code. My applications seem to be less buggy and work more quickly the less code I write!) Nevertheless, to write a production application, you'll typically need to react to events, provide custom decision logic, or include many other non-UI operations, so you'll need to mix XAML and code. Fortunately, this is extremely easy to do.

I'll describe XAML files in more depth in Chapter 3; for now, let's look at a primer for XAML:

- A *XAML element name* is a .NET Framework class name. When you define a XAML element, you are effectively creating an instance of the .NET Framework class with the same name as the XAML element.

- A *XAML attribute name* maps to the property or field with the same name, typically in the class instance.

In the SimpleApplication1.cs program, I create a window and add some controls to it by using the following code:

```
// Create the application's main window
mainWindow = new MSAvalon.Windows.Window ();

// Add a dark red, 14 point, "Hello World!" text element
txtElement = new MSAvalon.Windows.Controls.SimpleText ();
txtElement.Text = "Hello World!";
txtElement.Foreground = new
        MSAvalon.Windows.Media.SolidColorBrush (Colors.DarkRed);
txtElement.FontSize = new FontSize (14, FontSizeType.Point);
mainWindow.Children.Add (txtElement);
mainWindow.Show ();
```

The following XAML document produces exactly this same UI.

HelloWorld.xaml

```
<Window xmlns="http://schemas.microsoft.com/2003/xaml" Visible="true">
    <SimpleText Foreground="DarkRed" FontSize="14">Hello World!</SimpleText>
</Window>
```

The root *Window* element creates an instance of a class named *MSAvalon.Windows.Window*. Somehow, the build system needs to know that the XAML element named *Window* refers to an instance of the class named *MSAvalon.Windows.Window*. The *xmlns* attribute value provides this mapping.

XML parsers interpret unqualified element names relative to the namespace specified in the most-recent, in-scope, default namespace attribute, *xmlns*. When you specify an *xmlns* value of *"http://schemas.microsoft.com/ 2003/xaml"*, the build system interprets an unqualified element name on the defining element, or one of its subordinate elements, as the name of a class in a predefined set of namespaces.

Let me restate that in more concrete terms, using C# as an example. The *xmlns* declaration effectively adds a number of *using* statements to your code. The build system then interprets each unqualified XAML element name as a class name with the *using* declarations providing the context for the possible namespaces. Although the list might change, at the time of this writing, specifying the standard value for the default namespace attribute causes inclusion of the following *using* statements:

```
using MSAvalon.Windows;
using MSAvalon.Windows.Controls;
using MSAvalon.Windows.Controls.Primitives;
using MSAvalon.Windows.Data;
using MSAvalon.Windows.Documents;
using MSAvalon.Windows.Shapes;
using MSAvalon.Windows.Media;
using MSAvalon.Windows.Media.Animation;
using MSAvalon.Windows.Navigation;
```

The standard default namespace declaration also causes the build system to reference the *PresentationFramework* and *PresentationCore* assemblies, which contain classes in the previously listed namespaces.

I set the *Visible* attribute of the *Window* element to *true*. This corresponds to my original code that displays the window by calling its *Show* method.

I've nested a *SimpleText* element within the *Window* element definition. This tells the system to instantiate an *MSAvalon.Windows.Controls.SimpleText* object, make it a child of the *Window* object, and set the value of the simple text object to the *"Hello World!"* string.

Save the preceding XAML code in a file named HelloWorld.xaml, and run the file. The browser will interpret the XAML code in the file and display the UI, as shown in Figure 1-1.

Figure 1-1   The browser displaying the XAML version of Hello World

You might want to use a .NET class that isn't defined in one of the default namespaces listed previously. A typical example is using a class from an assembly that you create. The build system needs to be able to map the element name that you specify in the XAML source file to the appropriate .NET class in the correct assembly. XAML defines an XML processing instruction (PI) named *?Mapping* that you use to make this association.

The *?Mapping* PI allows you to define an XML namespace prefix that maps to a CLR namespace and assembly. When you qualify an XAML element name with this namespace prefix, you tell the build system, in effect, to take the element name, add the CLR prefix to the name, and create an instance of the class with the resulting name. The compiler will reference the specified assembly so that it can find the definition of the class.

The following example creates an instance of the *WiseOwl.Statistics.PoissonDeviate* class, the definition of which resides in the *WiseOwl.Statistics.Library* assembly:

```
<?Mapping XmlNamespace="stat" ClrNamespace="WiseOwl.Statistics"
                         Assembly="WiseOwl.Statistics.Library" ?>
<Window xmlns="http://schemas.microsoft.com/2003/xaml" Visible="true">
    <SimpleText Foreground="DarkRed" FontSize="14">Hello World!</SimpleText>
    <stat:PoissonDeviate Mean="5.0" />
</Window>
```

I cannot emphasize enough that XAML is simply another way to produce code that uses the .NET Framework UI classes. In fact, you could have a tool that displays a XAML UI specification graphically using a visual designer. Another tool might do the reverse and allow you to design the UI graphically and save it as a XAML file. Yet another tool might save the UI design as procedural code, which is similar to how the WinForms designer works. All these approaches are just different methods of specifying the same information.

Earlier in this chapter, I mentioned that the browser could render a XAML file in its window. The browser can do this only when the XAML file contains nothing but markup, like the simple example just shown. As your UI becomes more complicated, you'll typically have to use event handlers and other non-markup source code in addition to the XAML that describes the UI. Any time you have a mixed source code base—that is, markup and nonmarkup source code—you must compile the markup and source code using the MSBuild utility. After compilation, you can run the application as a stand-alone component or have the browser display the resulting UI.

Summary

All right! You now understand the basics of the new application model. You've learned how to use markup to create a UI declaratively, albeit a very simple UI. You could write the equivalent of Web pages using XAML files and deploy those files to a server for a user to browse. However, scenarios that are more interesting will typically require you to compile the application before deploying it. So let's jump right in and learn how to build and deploy a Longhorn application.

2

Building a Longhorn Application

To build a Longhorn application, you need the Longhorn Software Development Kit (SDK) installed. Alternatively, you can install a Microsoft Visual Studio release that supports Longhorn. In this book, I don't discuss using Visual Studio because its wizards, fancy code generation features, and project build capabilities obscure what actually happens under the covers. I believe that you should understand what a tool does for you before you rely on the tool.

When you install the Longhorn SDK, it creates a set of Start menu items that you can use to create a command prompt session in which you can build Longhorn applications. To build Debug versions of your application on a Microsoft Windows XP 32-bit system, navigate through the following menu items to create the appropriate command prompt session:

- Start
- Programs
- Microsoft Longhorn SDK
- Open Build Environment Window
- Windows XP 32-bit Build Environment
- Set Windows XP 32-bit Build Environment (Debug).

The Microsoft .NET Build Engine—MSBuild.exe

MSBuild is the primary tool you use to build a Longhorn application. You can run MSBuild with the help command-line option to get detailed information on its usage:

```
MSBuild /?
```

When you execute MSBuild without any command-line arguments, as shown here, it searches in the current working directory for a file name that ends with "proj", for example, .proj, .csproj, etc. When it finds one, it builds the project according to the directives in that file.

```
MSBuild
```

When you have more than one project file in the directory, you can specify the appropriate project file on the command line:

```
MSBuild <ProjectName>.proj
```

Normally, MSBuild builds the default target in the project file. You can override this and specify the target you want build. For example, to build the target named *CleanBuild*, you invoke MSBuild as follows:

```
MSBuild /t:Cleanbuild
```

Building Hello World Using MSBuild

Let's look at the files necessary to create a simple navigation-based Hello World application. Later I'll describe the purpose and use of each file in detail.

First, you need to define the *Application* object. You do this in a file typically called the *application definition file*. This HelloWorldApplication.xaml file defines my *Application* object.

HelloWorldApplication.xaml

```
<NavigationApplication xmlns="http://schemas.microsoft.com/2003/xaml"
                       StartupUri="HelloWorld.xaml" />
```

This definition says, "For my *Application* object, I want to use an instance of the *MSAvalon.Windows.Navigation.NavigationApplication* class. On startup, the application should navigate to and display the user interface (UI) defined in the HelloWorld.xaml file."

Here are the contents of the HelloWorld.xaml file. It's a slightly more interesting version of the previous Hello World example in Chapter 1.

HelloWorld.xaml

```xml
<Border xmlns="http://schemas.microsoft.com/2003/xaml">
  <FlowPanel>
    <SimpleText Foreground="DarkRed" FontSize="14">Hello World!</SimpleText>
  </FlowPanel>
</Border>
```

Now that I have all the "code" for my simple Hello World application, I need a project file that defines how to build my application. Here's my HelloWorld.proj file.

HelloWorld.proj

```xml
<Project DefaultTargets="Build">
  <PropertyGroup>
    <Property Language="C#" />
    <Property DefaultClrNameSpace="IntroLonghorn" />
    <Property TargetName="HelloWorld" />
  </PropertyGroup>

  <!--Imports the target which contains all the common targets-->
  <Import Project="$(LAPI)\WindowsApplication.target" />

  <ItemGroup>
    <!-- Application markup -->
    <Item Type="ApplicationDefinition" Include="HelloWorldApplication.xaml" />

    <!-- Compiled Xaml Files list -->
    <Item Type="Pages" Include="HelloWorld.xaml"/>
  </ItemGroup>
</Project>
```

Put these three files in a directory. Open a Longhorn SDK command prompt, navigate to the directory containing your files, and run MSBuild. It will compile your program into an executable.

We'll examine the contents of the application definition file later in this chapter. In Chapter 3, I describe in detail many of the Extensible Application Markup Language (XAML) elements you can use to define a UI. Before we look at the project file in more depth, let's review some MSBuild terminology.

MSBuild Terminology

Let's establish definitions for some MSBuild elements. A *Property* is a key-value pair. A *Property*'s value can originate from an environment variable, from a command-line switch, or from a *Property* definition in a project file, as shown here:

```
<Property OutputDir="bin\" />
```

You can think of an *Item* as an array of files. An *Item* can contain wild-cards and can exclude specific files. MSBuild uses the *Type* attribute of an *Item* to categorize items, as shown here:

```
<Item Type="Compile" Include="*.cs" Exclude="DebugStuff.cs" />
```

A *Task* is an atomic unit in the build process. A *Task* can accept input parameters from *Property* elements, *Item* elements, or plain strings. The *Name* of a *Task* identifies the build .NET data type required to perform the *Task*. A *Task* can emit *Item*s that other *Task*s consume. MSBuild includes many tasks, all of which can be broadly categorized as

- .NET tool tasks
- Deployment tasks
- Shell tasks

For example, the *Task* with a *Name* of *Csc* invokes the C# compiler as the build tool, which compiles all *Item* elements specified in the *Sources* attribute (which specifies *Item* elements with a *Type* of *Compile*) into an assembly, and produces the assembly as an output *Item*.

```
<Task Name="Csc" AssemblyName="$(OutputDir)\HelloWorld.exe"
             Sources="@(Compile)" />
```

A *Target* is a single logical step in the build process. A *Target* can perform timestamp analysis. This means that a *Target* will not run if it's not required. A *Target* executes one or more *Task*s to perform the desired operations, as shown here:

```
<Target Name="CopyToServer"
        Inputs="$(OutputDir)\HelloWorld.exe"
        Outputs="\\DeployServer\$(BuildNum)\HelloWorld.exe"
        DependsOnTargets="Compile">

  <Task Name="Copy" ... />
</Target>
```

A *Condition* attribute is roughly equivalent to a simple *if* statement. A *Condition* can compare two strings or check for the existence of a file or directory. You can apply a *Condition* to any element in a project file. For example, here's a group of properties that are defined only when the *Configuration* property has the value *Debug*:

```
<PropertyGroup Condition=" '$(Configuration)'=='Debug' " >
    <Property ... />
    <Property ... />
</PropertyGroup>
```

An *Import* is roughly equivalent to a C/C++ *#include* statement, as shown in the following example. When you import a project, the contents of the imported project logically become a part of the importing project.

```
<Import Project="$(LAPI)\WindowsApplication.target" />
```

Now that the terminology is out of the way, let's examine a typical project file.

Building a Longhorn Executable Application

Here's a simple, but relatively comprehensive, project file that builds an executable Longhorn application:

```
<Project DefaultTargets="Build">
  <PropertyGroup>
    <Property Language="C#" />
    <Property DefaultClrNameSpace="IntroLonghorn" />
    <Property TargetName="MyApp" />
  </PropertyGroup>

  <Import Project="$(LAPI)\WindowsApplication.target" />

  <ItemGroup>
    <Item Type="ApplicationDefinition" Include="MyApp.xaml" />

    <Item Type="Pages" Include="HomePage.xaml" />
    <Item Type="Pages" Include="DetailPage.xaml" />
    <Item Type="Code" Include="DetailPage.xaml.cs"/>

    <Item Type="DependentProjects" Include="MyDependentAssembly.proj" />

    <Item Type="Components" Include="SomeThirdParty.dll" />

    <Item Type="Resources" Include="Picture1.jpg"
          FileStorage="embedded" Localizable="False"/>
```

```
    <Item Type="Resources" Include="Picture2.jpg"
          FileStorage="embedded" Localizable="True"/>
  </ItemGroup>
</Project>
```

The *Project* Element

All project files begin with a root element definition named *Project*. Its *Default-Targets* attribute specifies the names of the targets that the system should build when you don't otherwise specify a target. In this example, I specify that, by default, the system should build the target named *Build*.

The *PropertyGroup* and *Property* Elements

Build rules can conditionally execute based on property values. As mentioned, a property's value can originate from an environment variable, from an MSBuild command-line switch, or from a property definition in a project file.

A project for an application must specify, at a minimum, a value for the *Language* and *TargetName* properties. In this example, I specify that the language is C# and that the name of the resulting application should be *MyApp*. I've also assigned a value to the property named *DefaultClrNameSpace*.

The build system compiles each XAML file into a managed class definition. By default, the managed class will have the same name as the base file name of the XAML source file. For example, the file Markup.xaml compiles into a definition of a class named *Markup*. By setting the *DefaultClrNameSpace* property to *IntroLonghorn*, I'm asking the build system to prefix generated class names with the *IntroLonghorn* namespace. Because of this, the build system produces a class named *IntroLonghorn.Markup* for the Markup.xaml definition.

I defined my properties prior to importing other projects, so the rules in the imported projects will use my specified property values—for example, I'll get the proper build rules for C# applications because I define the *Language* property as *C#*.

The *Import* Element

The rules in the *Build* target produce my Longhorn application's executable file. Specifying those build rules in every project file would be tedious and repetitive. So a little later in the project file, I use the following definition to import a predefined project file named *WindowsApplication.target*:

```
<Import Project="$(LAPI)\WindowsApplication.target" />
```

This imported file contains the standard build rules for building a Windows application, and it (indirectly) defines the target named *Build*.

The *ItemGroup* and *Item* Elements

The *ItemGroup* element and its child *Item* elements define all the parts required to build the application.

You must have one *Item* with a *Type* of *ApplicationDefinition*, as shown here. This *Item* specifies the file that describes the *Application* object to use for your application. The *Application* object is typically an instance of either the *MSAvalon.Windows.Application* class or the *MSAvalon.Windows.Navigation.NavigationApplication* class, both of which I describe later in this chapter.

```
<Item Type="ApplicationDefinition" Include="MyApp.xaml" />
```

Each *Item* with a *Type* of *Pages* defines a set of XAML files, as shown here. The build system compiles these XAML definitions into classes that it includes in the resulting assembly.

```
<Item Type="Pages" Include="HomePage.xaml" />
<Item Type="Pages" Include="DetailPage.xaml" />
```

Each *Item* with a *Type* of *Code* represents a source file, as shown here. The build system compiles these source files using the appropriate compiler selected by your project's *Language* property.

```
<Item Type="Code" Include="DetailPage.xaml.cs"/>
```

This project might depend on other projects. The build system must compile these dependent projects before it can build this project. You list each such dependent project using an *Item* with *Type* of *DependentProjects*:

```
<Item Type="DependentProjects" Include="MyDependentAssembly.proj" />
```

Code in this project might use types in a prebuilt assembly, also known as a *component assembly*. To compile code using such component assemblies, the compiler needs a reference to each assembly. In addition, when you deploy your application, you will need to deploy these component assemblies as well. You list each component assembly using an *Item* with *Type* of *Components*:

```
<Item Type="Components" Include="SomeThirdParty.dll" />
```

A referenced assembly is somewhat different from a component assembly. In both cases, your code uses types in a prebuilt assembly. However, you don't ship a referenced assembly as part of your application, whereas you do ship a component assembly as part of your application. The build system needs to know this distinction.

You specify an *Item* with a *Type* of *References* to indicate that the compiler must reference the specified assembly at build time, as shown here, but the assembly will not be part of the application deployment. The build system automatically includes references to standard system assemblies—for example, mscorlib.dll, System.dll, PresentationFramework.dll. and more—but you'll have to add any nonstandard assembly your application must reference.

```
<Item Type="References" Include="SharedThirdParty.dll" />
```

Your application might also use resources. An *Item* with a *Type* of *Resources* describes a resource used by the application, as shown here. The build system can embed the resource into the resulting assembly or include it as a stand-alone file. The build system can also place localizable resources into satellite assemblies.

```
<Item Type="Resources" Include="Picture1.jpg"
      FileStorage="embedded" Localizable="False"/>
<Item Type="Resources" Include="Picture2.jpg"
      FileStorage="embedded" Localizable="True"/>
```

Building a Longhorn Library Assembly

You'll also want to build libraries in addition to executable applications. The primary differences between an application project and a library project are these:

- A library project sets the value of the *TargetType* property to *Library*.

- A library project typically does not include an application definition item.

Here's an example of a project file that creates a library:

```
<Project DefaultTargets="Build">
  <PropertyGroup>
    <Property Language="C#" />
    <Property DefaultClrNameSpace="IntroLonghorn" />
    <Property TargetName="MyLibrary" />
    <Property TargetType="Library" />
  </PropertyGroup>

  <Import Project="$(LAPI)\WindowsApplication.target" />

  <ItemGroup>
    <Item Type="Pages" Include="ErrorPage.xaml" />
    <Item Type="Code" Include="ErrorPage.xaml.cs"/>
    <Item Type="Code" Include="Utilities.cs"/>
```

```
  <Item Type="DependentProjects" Include="MyDependentAssembly.proj" />

  <Item Type="Components" Include="SomeThirdParty.dll" />

  <Item Type="Resources" Include="Picture1.jpg"
        FileStorage="embedded" Localizable="False"/>
  <Item Type="Resources" Include="Picture2.jpg"
        FileStorage="embedded" Localizable="True"/>
 </ItemGroup>
</Project>
```

Building a Longhorn Document

You aren't restricted to building applications with XAML. You can also use XAML files to create a highly interactive, intelligently rendered, adaptive document for a user to read. In this case, your XAML files collectively represent pages of a document. You can use the MSBuild engine to build such documents.

The changes to the project file to build a document instead of an application are minor:

- Set the value of the *TargetType* property to *Document*.
- Import the WindowsDocument.target project for the appropriate build rules.
- Include all other project files as usual.

It's important to understand what a *TargetType* of *Document* really produces. When you build a *Document*, the build output is a .container file, and the build system optimizes the contents of the container for download rather than speed. A container file is an extension of the Windows Structured Storage, also known as DocFile, format. Longhorn container handling provides features that allow rendering of partially downloaded files. Therefore, you don't need the entire container downloaded before the application starts running.

In addition, when you ask MSBuild to create a container file, it compiles each XAML file into a binary representation of the XML, called binary XAML (BAML). BAML is far more compact than either the original text file or a compiled-to-IL assembly. BAML files download more quickly—are optimized for download—but an interpreter must parse them at run time to create instances of the classes described in the file. Therefore, such files are not optimized for speed. Up to now, I've been generating compiled-to-IL files (also known as CAML files, short for compiled XAML).

Here's an example of a project file that creates an electronic document:

```
<Project DefaultTargets="Build">
  <PropertyGroup>
    <Property TargetType="Document" />
     <Property Language="C#" />
     <Property DefaultClrNameSpace="IntroLonghorn" />
     <Property TargetName="MyDocument" />
  </PropertyGroup>

  <Import Project="$(LAPI)\WindowsDocument.target" />

  <ItemGroup>
    <Item Type="ApplicationDefinition" Include="MyApp.xaml" />

    <Item Type="Pages" Include="Markup.xaml" />
    <Item Type="Pages" Include="Navigate.xaml" />
    <Item Type="Code" Include="Navigate.xaml.cs"/>

    <Item Type="Resources" Include="Picture1.jpg"
        FileStorage="embedded" Localizable="False"/>
    <Item Type="Resources" Include="Picture2.jpg"
        FileStorage="embedded" Localizable="True"/>
  </ItemGroup>
</Project>
```

Now that you've learned how to build the various types of Longhorn applications and components, let's look at XAML files in more detail. Specifically, let's look at what the build system does when it turns a XAML file into a .NET class.

A XAML File as a Class Declaration

The application definition file is the XAML file that defines the class of your application's *Application* object. However, in general, a XAML document is simply a file that defines a class. The class produced by the XAML definition derives from the class associated with the XML document's root element name. By default, the build system uses the XAML base file name as the generated class name.

Creating an Application Definition File for a Navigation Application

Recall that the *Item* element with *Type* of *ApplicationDefinition* specifies the name of the XAML file that defines the *Application* object. In other words, this element specifies the XAML file that contains the entry point for your application. The Longhorn platform will create an instance of the *MSAvalon.Windows.Application*-derived type that you define in this file and let it manage the startup, shutdown, and navigation of your application.

In Chapter 1, you saw how to create and use an application instance programmatically. The following XAML file uses markup to define the *Application* object for a project:

```
<NavigationApplication xmlns="http://schemas.microsoft.com/2003/xaml"
                       StartupUri="HelloWorld.xaml" />
```

I expect that most Longhorn applications will be navigation-based applications and, therefore, will often just reuse the standard *NavigationApplication* object. You can reuse this application definition file for most of your navigation-based applications by changing only the value of the *StartupUri* attribute.

For example, if the previous application definition resides in the HelloWorldApplication.xaml file and I use the HelloWorld.proj project file listed previously, the build system produces the following class declaration:

```
namespace IntroLonghorn {
  class HelloWorldApplication :
          MSAvalon.Windows.Navigation.NavigationApplication {
      ⋮
    }
  }
```

The namespace results from the *DefaultClrNameSpace* declaration in the project file, the declared class name is the same as the base file name, and the declared class extends the class represented by the root element in the XAML file.

Customizing the Generated Code Using Attributes

When you declare a root element in a XAML file, you can use attributes on the root element to control the name of the generated class declaration. You can use any of the following optional attributes:

- A namespace prefix definition that associates a prefix with a namespace named *Definition*. You must define a prefix for this namespace to use the *Language* and *Class* attributes. Traditionally, the *def* prefix is used.

- A *Language* attribute (defined in the *Definition* namespace) that specifies the programming language used by any inline code in the XAML file.

- A *Class* attribute (defined in the *Definition* namespace) that specifies the name of the generated class. When you specify a name containing one or more periods, the build system does not prefix the name with the *DefaultClrNameSpace* value.

As an example, let's change the contents of the HelloWorldApplication.xaml file to the following:

```
<NavigationApplication xmlns="http://schemas.microsoft.com/2003/xaml"
                       xmlns:def="Definition"
                       def:Class="Special.MyApp"
                       def:CodeBehind="HelloWorldApplication.xaml.cs"
                       StartupUri="HelloWorld.xaml" />
```

The generated class would then be this:

```
namespace Special {
  class MyApp :
        MSAvalon.Windows.Navigation.NavigationApplication {
  ⋮
  }
}
```

Using Code and Markup in the Same Class

Nearly all applications will require you to write some code—for example, a click event handler for a button or a virtual method override—in addition to the markup that specifies the UI. Recall from Chapter 1 that my non-navigation-based application overrode the *OnStartingUp* method to create its window and controls. I'll rewrite that example to illustrate how you would combine application code and markup.

While this forthcoming example creates a non-navigation application, I want to emphasize that there is really no compelling reason to create such an application. You can always create a navigation-based application that never actually navigates to a different page. However, writing such an application requires me to mix code and markup in the same class therefore provides a good example.

Recall that creating a non-navigation application requires you to define a custom class that inherits from *MSAvalon.Windows.Application* and that overrides the *OnStartingUp* method. The application definition file declares the application object class that your program uses. Therefore, a non-navigation application must define its overriding *OnStartingUp* method in the same class.

Except for the following changes, an application configuration file for a non-navigation application contains the same items as a definition file for a navigation application:

- The root element is *Application* instead of *NavigationApplication*.

- The file must contain or reference the implementation of the *OnStartingUp* method for your application class.

Because I need to use markup and code to implement a single class, I need to show you a technique to associate a source code file with a XAML file.

Associating a Source-Behind File with a XAML File

You will frequently want to develop portions of your application by using markup and to develop other parts by using a more traditional programming language. I strongly recommend separating the UI and the logic into individual source files by using the following technique.

You can add a XAML *CodeBehind* element (defined in the *Definition* namespace) to the root element of any XAML file and specify the name of a source code file (also known as the *code-behind file*). The build engine will compile the XAML declarations into a managed class. The build system also compiles the code-behind file into a managed class declaration. The tricky aspect is that both of these class declarations represent partial declarations of a single class.

Here's a XAML definition that produces a non-navigation application class equivalent to the first example in Chapter 1:

```
<Application xmlns="http://schemas.microsoft.com/2003/xaml"
             xmlns:def="Definition"
             def:Language="C#"
             def:Class="IntroLonghorn.CodeBehindSample"
             def:CodeBehind="CodeBehind.xaml.cs" />
```

There are two noteworthy aspects to this application definition file:

- The *Language* attribute specifies that the code-behind file contains C# source code.

- The *CodeBehind* attribute specifies that the source file name is CodeBehindMySample2.xaml.cs.

Here's the matching source-behind file:

```
namespace IntroLonghorn {
  using System;
  using MSAvalon.Windows;
```

```
using MSAvalon.Windows.Controls;
using MSAvalon.Windows.Media;

public partial class CodeBehindSample {
  MSAvalon.Windows.Controls.SimpleText txtElement;
  MSAvalon.Windows.Window              mainWindow;

  protected override
  void OnStartingUp (StartingUpCancelEventArgs e) {
    base.OnStartingUp (e);
    CreateAndShowMainWindow ();
  }

  private void CreateAndShowMainWindow () {
    // Create the application's main window
    mainWindow = new MSAvalon.Windows.Window ();

    // Add a dark red, 14 point, "Hello World!" text element
    txtElement = new MSAvalon.Windows.Controls.SimpleText ();
    txtElement.Text = "Hello World!";
    txtElement.Foreground = new
     MSAvalon.Windows.Media.SolidColorBrush (Colors.DarkRed);
    txtElement.FontSize = new FontSize (14,
                                        FontSizeType.Point);
    mainWindow.Children.Add (txtElement);
    mainWindow.Show ();
  }
 }
}
```

Notice the *partial* keyword in the class declaration in the code-behind file. This keyword states that the compiler should merge this class definition with other definitions of the same class. This allows you to provide multiple partial definitions of a class, each in a separate source file, that the compiler combines into a single class definition in the resulting assembly.

Mixing Source Code and Markup in a Single XAML File

I think it's just wrong to mix source code and markup in the same file. I even considered not showing you how to do it. However, some evildoer somewhere will write a sample program using this technique, so you might need to understand what he has done. Moreover, you can then use the code-behind file approach described previously to rid the world of a small amount of evil and separate the UI from the logic.

Here's an application definition file with the source code inserted directly inline with the markup:

```xml
<Application xmlns="http://schemas.microsoft.com/2003/xaml"
    xmlns:def="Definition"
    def:Language="C#"
    def:Class="IntroLonghorn.MySample2" >

  <def:Code>
  <![CDATA[
    protected override void OnStartingUp (StartingUpCancelEventArgs e) {
      base.OnStartingUp (e);
      CreateAndShowMainWindow ();
    }
    . . . Remaining methods elided for clarity
  ]]>
  </def:Code>
</Application>
```

In this example, the *Language* attribute specifies that the inline source code is C#. Notice that the *Code* element is a CDATA block containing the inline source code. It's sometimes technically necessary to enclose inline source code in an XML CDATA block to ensure that the document is well-formed. In fact, the XAML parser always requires you to enclose the inline source code in a CDATA block, even when omitting it produces a well-formed document.

I apologize once again for showing you such a travesty.

The Application Manifest

When you compile an application, MSBuild produces the .exe file plus two manifest files: the application manifest, *.manifest, and a deployment manifest, *.deploy. You use these manifests when deploying an application or document from a server. First, copy the application, all of its dependencies, and the two manifest files to the appropriate location on your server. Second, edit the deployment manifest so that it points to the location of the application manifest.

For completeness, let's look at examples of the application and deployment manifests. The application manifest, shown in the following example, is actually not as interesting as the deployment manifest. The application manifest simply defines all the parts that make up an application. MSBuild produces the application manifest when it builds your application, and you typically modify little or nothing in it.

HelloWorld.manifest

```xml
<?xml version="1.0" encoding="utf-8"?>
<assembly xmlns="urn:schemas-microsoft-com:asm.v1" manifestVersion="1.0"
        xmlns:asmv2="urn:schemas-microsoft-com:asm.v2"
        xmlns:xsi="http://www.w3.org/2001/XMLSchema-instance"
    xsi:schemaLocation="urn:schemas-microsoft-com:asm.v1 assembly.adaptive.xsd">
```

```
<assemblyIdentity name="HelloWorld" version="1.0.0.0"
                  processorArchitecture="x86" asmv2:culture="en-us"
                  publicKeyToken="0000000000000000" />

<entryPoint name="main" xmlns="urn:schemas-microsoft-com:asm.v2"
            dependencyName="HelloWorld">

  <commandLine file="HelloWorld.exe" parameters="" />
</entryPoint>

<TrustInfo xmlns="urn:schemas-microsoft-com:asm.v2" xmlns:temp="temporary">
  <Security>
    <ApplicationRequestMinimum>
      <PermissionSet class="System.Security.PermissionSet" version="1"
                     ID="SeeDefinition">
        <IPermission
          class="System.Security.Permissions.FileDialogPermission"
          version="1" Unrestricted="true" />
        <IPermission
          class="System.Security.Permissions.IsolatedStorageFilePermission"
          version="1" Allowed="DomainIsolationByUser" UserQuota="5242880" />
        <IPermission
          class="System.Security.Permissions.SecurityPermission"
          version="1" Flags="Execution" />
        <IPermission
          class="System.Security.Permissions.UIPermission" version="1"
          Window="SafeTopLevelWindows" Clipboard="OwnClipboard" />
        <IPermission
          class="System.Security.Permissions.PrintingPermission"
          version="1" Level="SafePrinting" />
        <IPermission
          class="MSAvalon.Windows.AVTempUIPermission, PresentationFramework,
                 Version=6.0.4030.0, Culture=neutral,
                 PublicKeyToken=a29c01bbd4e39ac5" version="1"
                 NewWindow="LaunchNewWindows" FullScreen="SafeFullScreen" />
      </PermissionSet>

      <AssemblyRequest name="HelloWorld"
                       PermissionSetReference="SeeDefinition" />
    </ApplicationRequestMinimum>
  </Security>
</TrustInfo>

<dependency asmv2:name="HelloWorld">
  <dependentAssembly>
    <assemblyIdentity name="HelloWorld" version="0.0.0.0"
                      processorArchitecture="x86" />
  </dependentAssembly>
```

```
      <asmv2:installFrom codebase="HelloWorld.exe"
                         hash="5c58153494c16296d9cab877136c3f106785bfab"
                         hashalg="SHA1" size="5632" />
   </dependency>
</assembly>
```

Most of the contents of the application manifest should be relatively obvious. The *entryPoint* element specifies the name of the entry point method, *main*, and references the *dependency*, named *HelloWorld*, that contains the entry point. The *entryPoint* element also contains the program name and command-line argument that the shell will need to run the application.

The *HelloWorld dependency* element contains the information (the *dependentAssembly* element) that specifies the dependent assembly and an *installFrom* element that tells the loader where to find the assembly's file and the file's original hash. The loader can use the hash to detect changes made to the assembly subsequent to compilation.

The Longhorn Trust Manager uses the *TrustInfo* element to determine the security permissions that the application requires. In the previous example, my HelloWorld application defines a set of permissions it names the *SeeDefinition* permission set. Immediately after I define the set of permissions, the *AssemblyRequest* element requests that the assembly named *HelloWorld* receives at least the set of permissions in the set named *SeeDefinition*. The permissions in this example are the permissions normally granted to applications running in the SEE, so the Hello World application runs without displaying to the user any Trust Manager security warnings.

The Deployment Manifest

As mentioned, the deployment manifest is more interesting. The deployment manifest contains, obviously enough, settings that control the deployment of the application.

HelloWorld.deploy

```
<?xml version="1.0" encoding="UTF-8" standalone="yes"?>
<assembly xmlns="urn:schemas-microsoft-com:asm.v1" manifestVersion="1.0"
          xmlns:asmv2="urn:schemas-microsoft-com:asm.v2"
          xmlns:xsi="http://www.w3.org/2001/XMLSchema-instance"
   xsi:schemaLocation="urn:schemas-microsoft-com:asm.v1 assembly.adaptive.xsd">

   <assemblyIdentity name="HelloWorld.deploy" version="1.0.0.0"
                     processorArchitecture="x86" asmv2:culture="en-us"
                     publicKeyToken="0000000000000000" />
```

```
<description asmv2:publisher="Wise Owl, Inc."
             asmv2:product="Brent's HelloWorld Application"
  asmv2:supportUrl="http://www.wiseowl.com/AppServer/HelloWorld/support.asp"
/>

<deployment xmlns="urn:schemas-microsoft-com:asm.v2"
            isRequiredUpdate="false">
  <install shellVisible="true" />
  <subscription>
    <update>
      <beforeApplicationStartup />
      <periodic>
        <minElapsedTimeAllowed time="6" unit="hours" />
        <maxElapsedTimeAllowed time="1" unit="weeks" />
      </periodic>
    </update>
  </subscription>
</deployment>
<dependency>
  <dependentAssembly>
    <assemblyIdentity name="HelloWorld" version="1.0.0.0"
                      processorArchitecture="x86" asmv2:culture="en-us"
                      publicKeyToken="0000000000000000" />
  </dependentAssembly>
  <asmv2:installFrom codebase="HelloWorld.manifest" />
</dependency>
</assembly>
```

The deployment manifest contains information that Longhorn requires to install and update an application. Notice that the *assemblyIdentity* element of the deployment manifest references the application manifest. After all, the application manifest already describes all the components of an application. To install an application, the deployment manifest says, in effect, "Here's the description of the files you need to install this application."

Of course, when you install an application, you also need more information than just the files to copy onto a system. The *description* element lists the *publisher*, *product*, and *supportUrl* attributes; the system displays their contents in the Add/Remove Programs dialog box.

The *deployment* element specifies how to deploy and update the application after deployment. In this example, the application is visible to the shell, and the client's system will check for and, if necessary, download a new version of the application each time the user starts the application. In addition, the system periodically—no more than every six hours and no less than once a week—checks for a new version. When the periodic check locates a new version, Longhorn will download the new version in the background and install it; it will then be ready to run the next time the user executes the application.

Running the Application

Normally, a user will "run" the application manifest to execute the application from the server directly without installing the application on the local computer. Longhorn downloads the components of the application as needed. In this case, the server must be available to run the application.

When a user "runs" the deployment manifest, Longhorn downloads and installs the application on the local computer. The application can install icons on the desktop, add Start menu items, and generally become a traditional installed application. Of course, you also get the automatic background updates, version rollback, and uninstall support.

When you first launch a deployment manifest, Longhorn installs the application in the application cache and adds an entry to the Control Panel's Add or Remove Programs list. Subsequently, whenever you run the deployment manifest, the application loads directly from the application cache. It is typically not downloaded again.

However, when you uninstall the application from the cache using the Control Panel's Add/Remove Programs applet, subsequently execution of the deployment manifest downloads and installs the application once again.

Alternatively, you can change the version number of the application on the server. Then, when you run the deployment manifest, Longhorn will download and install the new version side-by-side with the current version. Both versions of the application will appear in the Add or Remove Programs list.

Why Create Yet Another Build System?

I really like MSBuild, even though, at the time of this writing, I've had only a few weeks of experience with it. Of course, years of experience with makefiles makes any more elegant build system attractive. At present, there are two alternative build systems in common use—Make and Ant. It seems natural to compare MSBuild to such alternatives.

Why Not Use Make?

Why develop a new build system when many developers are familiar with an existing one called Make? Make has poor integration of tools into the build system. Make simply executes shell commands. Because of this, there's no inherent ability for one tool to communicate with another tool during the build process. MSBuild creates instances of the *Task* classes, and tasks can communicate among themselves passing normal .NET types.

Makefiles have an unusual syntax, are difficult to write, and don't scale well, as they get complex for large projects. In addition, tools other than Make cannot easily process a makefile. Tools other than MSBuild can easily generate and parse the XML-based syntax of an MSBuild project.

Finally, Make doesn't really have support for projects. There's no file system abstraction, and no support for cascading properties. Moreover, there's no design-time support for generating a makefile.

Why Not Use Ant?

A similar frequently asked question is why develop a new XML-based build system when there's an existing very successful and rich system called Ant? Ant is a Java, open source build system from *Apache.org* that pioneered XML-based project files and tasks as the atomic build operation. There's also a great .NET port of Ant called NAnt available from *nant.sourceforge.net*. On the surface, MSBuild and Ant/NAnt are similar. Both tools use XML as their project serialization format, and both tools use tasks as their atomic unit of build operation. Both tools have their strengths, but when you take a closer look they have different design goals.

Ant made the design decision to place much functionality into a large set of tasks. MSBuild has a different design goal, where similar functionality is encapsulated by the engine (such as timestamp analysis, intertask communication via items, task batching, item transforms, and so on). Both approaches have their strengths and weaknesses.

Ant's model allows developers to extend and control every detail of the build, and therefore it's very flexible. Nevertheless, it also puts a greater responsibility on task writers because tasks need to be much more sophisticated to provide consistent functionality. MSBuild's model lessens the amount of functionality that each task needs to implement. Project authors can therefore rely on consistent functionality across different projects, targets and tasks. In addition, integrated development environments such as Visual Studio can also rely on those services to provide consistent results and a rich user experience, without having to know anything about the internals of the tasks called during the build process.

Similarly, while Ant has the concept of a build script, it does not have the concept of a project manifest that MSBuild has. A build script says how to create a set of files but doesn't provide additional semantics describing how the files are used. A manifest additionally describes the semantics of the files, which allows additional tools, such as an IDE, to integrate more deeply with the build system. Conversely, the lack of a project manifest means a developer can more easily tailor Ant to build new kinds of "stuff" because there's no constraining schema for the build script.

Summary

You've now mastered the basics. You can write XAML and can compile, deploy, and run the resulting application. Unfortunately, the applications you've learned to write so far are pretty boring. Chapter 3 dives into XAML in depth and shows you how to use a wide variety of UI objects provided by the Longhorn platform. Later chapters show you a number of the other new technologies that you can also use in your applications.

3

Controls and XAML

As you've seen in Chapter 2, Longhorn platform applications typically consist of an *Application* object and a set of user interface pages that you write in a declarative markup language called XAML.

The *Application* object is a singleton and persists throughout the lifetime of the application. It allows your application logic to handle top-level events and share code and state among pages. The *Application* object also determines whether the application is a single window application or a navigation application.

You typically write each user interface page using a dialect of XML named Extensible Application Markup Language (XAML). Each page consists of XAML elements, text nodes, and other components organized in a hierarchical tree. The hierarchical relationship of these components determines how the page renders and behaves.

You can also consider a XAML page to be a description of an object model. When the runtime creates the page, it instantiates each of the elements and nodes described in the XAML document and creates an equivalent object model in memory. You can manipulate this object model programmatically—for example, you can add and remove elements and nodes to cause the page to render and behave differently.

Fundamentally, a XAML page describes the classes that the runtime should create, the property values and event handlers for the instances of the classes, and an object model hierarchy—that is, which instance is the parent of another instance.

All XAML documents are well-formed XML documents that use a defined set of element names. Therefore, all rules regarding the formation of well-formed XML documents apply equally to XAML documents. For example, the document must contain a single root element; all element names are case-sensitive; an element definition cannot overlap another element definition but must entirely contain it, and so on. If you're not familiar with XML syntax, now is an excellent time to learn it.

XAML Elements

Each XAML page contains one or more *elements* that control the layout and behavior of the page. You arrange these elements hierarchically in a tree. Every element has only one parent. Elements can generally have any number of child elements. However, some element types—for example, *Scrollbar*—have no children; and other element types—for example, *Border*—can have a single child element.

Each element name corresponds to the name of a managed class. Adding an element to a XAML document causes the runtime to create an instance of the corresponding class. For example, the following markup represents a root *DockPanel* element that has a single child *Table* element. The *Table* element contains three child *Row* elements. Each *Row* element contains three children, and a few of them have child text nodes.

```
<Border xmlns="http://schemas.microsoft.com/2003/xaml"
        Background="BlanchedAlmond">
  <DockPanel>
    <Table>
      <Body>
        <Row>
          <Cell><Button/></Cell>
          <Cell><Text>Item</Text></Cell>
          <Cell><Text>Price</Text></Cell>
        </Row>
        <Row>
          <Cell><CheckBox Checked="true"/></Cell>
          <Cell><TextBox Height="50">Nissan 350Z</TextBox></Cell>
          <Cell><TextBox Height="50">29.95</TextBox></Cell>
        </Row>
        <Row>
          <Cell><CheckBox/></Cell>
          <Cell><TextBox Height="50">Porsche Boxster</TextBox></Cell>
          <Cell><TextBox Height="50">9.95</TextBox></Cell>
        </Row>
      </Body>
    </Table>
  </DockPanel>
</Border>
```

This XAML document creates an object hierarchy as shown in Figure 3-1 and the display shown in Figure 3-2.

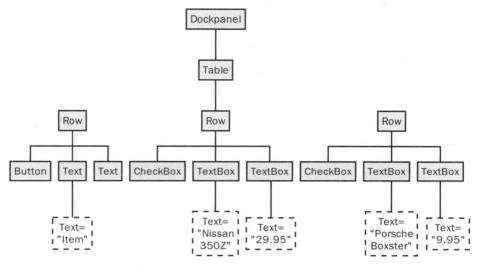

Figure 3-1   An example XAML page object model

Figure 3-2   The display from the previous XAML

You can access much of the functionality of such objects using only markup. Using only markup, you can do any of the following:

- Describe a hierarchical set of objects that the runtime will instantiate

- Set object properties to values known statically

- Set object properties to values retrieved from a data source

- Cause changed property values to be stored back into the data source

- Repeatedly change a property's value over time

- Bind an event handler to an object's event

However, although you can create some amazing user interfaces using only markup, you can also access an element's functionality programmatically using the XAML object model. The object model allows you to manipulate every aspect of the elements on a page. It actually provides additional capabilities that are not accessible through XAML.

Every XAML element derives from *System.Windows.UIElement* or *System.Windows.ContentElement*, and therefore all elements possess a number of common features. Elements can be grouped in the following four basic categories:

- *Controls* derive from *System.Windows.Control* and handle user interaction.

- *Panels* are specialized controls that derive from *System.Windows.Panel* and handle page layout and act as containers for elements.

- *Text formatting elements* derive from *System.Windows.TextElement* and handle text formatting and document structure.

- *Shapes* handle vector graphic shapes.

XAML Panels

A XAML page typically begins with a panel element. The panel is a container for a page's content and controls the positioning and rendering of that content. In fact, when you display anything using XAML, a panel is always involved, although sometimes it is implicit rather than one you describe explicitly. A panel can contain other panels, allowing you to partition the display surface into regions, each controlled by its panel.

There are six built-in *Panel* classes in the Longhorn platform:

- A *Canvas* positions each child element explicitly using coordinates relative to the *Canvas* area.

- A *DockPanel* puts its children in the top, bottom, left, right, or center of the panel. When you assign multiple children to the same area, a *DockPanel* arranges them either horizontally or vertically within that area.

- A *FlowPanel* arranges its child elements according to its line-breaking and alignment properties. When content exceeds the length of a single line, the panel will break lines, wrap lines, and align content appropriately.

- A *TextPanel* renders multiple lines of text in multiple text formats. You will typically use it only when you need complex text layout. For most cases, you'll use the lightweight *Text* element for basic text support.

- A *GridPanel* is a lightweight element that arranges its child elements in rows and columns forming a grid. It is useful for creating simple tables but has limited features. You would use the *Table* control for complex table layout.

- A *FixedPanel* positions its child elements on a fixed layout page. Elements on fixed layout pages always have the same positioning and pagination regardless of device resolution or window size.

Generally, these panels will provide sufficient functionality for most developers. However, you can also create your own panel classes that position and displays content in a specialized manner.

Canvas

The *Canvas* panel provides considerable flexibility regarding positioning and arranging elements on the screen. It allows you to specify the location for each child element and, when elements overlap, you can specify the order in which the canvas draws the overlapping elements by changing the order the elements appear in markup.

The following markup produces three overlapping graphics, as you see in Figure 3-1: a green rectangle with an orange border, a translucent yellow ellipse with a blue border, and some text centered in the rectangle.[1] The framework draws the shapes in the order presented, so the text appears over the rectangle.

```
<Canvas xmlns="http://schemas.microsoft.com/2003/xaml" >
  <Rectangle
    Fill="#33CC66"
    Width="2in"         Height="1in"
    Canvas.Top="25"              Canvas.Left="50"
    StrokeThickness="6px" Stroke="Orange" />

  <Ellipse
    Fill="yellow"
    CenterX="1.5in"      CenterY="1.1in"
    RadiusX=".5in"       RadiusY="1in"
    StrokeThickness="4px"   Stroke="Blue" />

   <Text
    Canvas.Top="50" Canvas.Left="60" Foreground="#000000"
    FontWeight="Bold" FontFamily="Arial"
    FontStyle="Normal" FontSize="25">Hello Shapes!</Text>

</Canvas>
```

1. The thought of never again writing a WM_PAINT handler to draw things like this brings tears to my eyes...tears of joy I hasten to add!

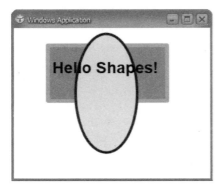

Figure 3-3   An example using the *Canvas* panel

DockPanel

The *DockPanel* panel arranges child elements horizontally or vertically, relative to each other. The *DockPanel* class examines the *Dock* property of each child element to determine how to align the element along the edges of the panel. You can set the *Dock* property to one of five values: *Top*, *Bottom*, *Left*, *Right*, or *Fill*.

For example, a panel aligns the first child element with its *Dock* property equal to *Top* against the top edge of the panel. The panel then aligns the next child element with its *Dock* property equal to *Top* just below the prior element. The panel similarly aligns child elements with their *Dock* property set to *Bottom*, *Left*, or *Right*. Setting the *Dock* property of the last child element to *Fill* causes it to occupy all remaining space in the *DockPanel*. Never follow a *Dock="Fill"* element with other elements because the subsequent elements will not be visible. The default value of the *Dock* property is *Left*, so when you do not set the *Dock* property for an element, it stacks horizontally to the left.

The *Dock* property is an attached property—it's defined by the *DockPanel* class, but you set it on a child element like this:

```
<child DockPanel.Dock="Top"/>
```

Or in code:

```
DockPanel.SetDock(child, Dock.Top)
```

The following markup uses a *DockPanel* and five *Canvas* panels to create a commonly seen user interface. The *DockPanel* aligns the first two canvases against the top of the *DockPanel*. It aligns the third canvas against the bottom edge of the *DockPanel*, the fourth against the left edge, and the fifth canvas fills the remaining space. You might put a menu in the top panel and a toolbar in the panel just below the menu. This decision leaves the left panel for a tree view, the bottom panel for a status bar, and the remaining panel for the detailed selected item view, as you can see in Figure 3-4.

```
<Border xmlns="http://schemas.microsoft.com/2003/xaml" Background="White">
  <DockPanel>
        <Border Width="500" DockPanel.Dock="Top" BorderThickness="2,2,2,2"
BorderBrush="Black" Background="#87ceeb" >
            <Text>Dock = "Top"</Text>
        </Border>
        <Border Width="500" DockPanel.Dock="Top" BorderThickness="2,2,2,2"
BorderBrush="Black" Background="#87ceeb" >
          <Text>Dock = "Top"</Text>
        </Border>
        <Border Width="500" DockPanel.Dock="Bottom" BorderThickness="2,2,2,2"
              BorderBrush="Black" Background="#ffff99" >
          <Text>Dock = "Bottom"</Text>
        </Border>
        <Border Width="200" DockPanel.Dock="Left" BorderThickness="2,2,2,2"
BorderBrush="Black" Background="#98fb98" >
          <Text>Dock = "Left"</Text>
        </Border>
        <Border Width="300" DockPanel.Dock="Fill" BorderThickness="2,2,2,2"
BorderBrush="Black" Background="White" >
          <Text>Dock = "Fill"</Text>
        </Border>
  </DockPanel>
</Border>
```

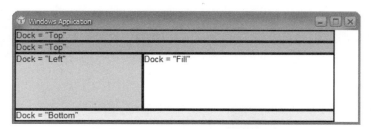

Figure 3-4   An example using the *DockPanel* panel

FlowPanel

The *FlowPanel* panel provides a number of automatic layout features and allows for complex presentations of text and graphics. You define the size of the panel using its *Width* and *Height* properties. The panel then displays its child elements in a way that best uses the panel's space, wrapping and aligning the elements as necessary. The default flow direction for a *FlowPanel* is from left to right and top to bottom.

The following markup example demonstrates how the *FlowPanel* breaks and wraps content. The *FlowPanel* contains four one-inch square canvases. The *FlowPanel* attempts to display its child elements left to right and top to bottom.

```
<Border xmlns="http://schemas.microsoft.com/2003/xaml" Background="White">
  <FlowPanel>
      <Border Background="Red" Width="1in" Height="1in"/>
      <Border Background="Green" Width="1in" Height="1in"/>
      <Border Background="Blue" Width="1in" Height="1in"/>
      <Border Background="Yellow" Width="1in" Height="1in"/>
  </FlowPanel>
</Border>
```

Figure 3-3 shows the output when the *FlowPanel* can fit all elements on a single line. Figure 3-4 demonstrates the *FlowPanel* wrapping the last element to a new line. Figure 3-5 shows the worst case where the *FlowPanel* must place each element on its own line. Figure 3-6 shows the last element wrapping to a new line, and Figure 3-7 shows every element wrapping to a new line.

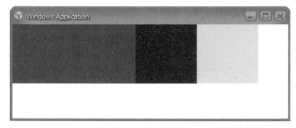

Figure 3-5   The *FlowPanel* breaks lines only when necessary.

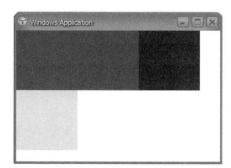

Figure 3-6   The *FlowPanel* panel wrapping the last element to a new line

Figure 3-7   The *FlowPanel* panel wrapping each element to a new line

TextPanel

The *TextPanel* panel formats, sizes, and draws text. This panel class supports multiple lines of text as well as multiple text formats. You will typically use the *TextPanel* class when you need complex layout support. However, when you require only simple text display, it's better to use the *Text* element instead.

The following markup example demonstrates how the *TextPanel* breaks and wraps content. The *TextPanel* adjusts the number of columns and the height of each column as you resize the window.

```
<Border xmlns="http://schemas.microsoft.com/2003/xaml" Background="White">
  <TextPanel
    ColumnCount="3"
    ColumnWidth="200px"
    ColumnGap="25px"
    ColumnRuleWidth="5px"
    ColumnRuleBrush="blue">

    <Block Background="LightGray">
      <Inline FontFamily="Arial" FontWeight="Bold"
            FontSize="16pt">Transcript of the
          <Italic>Nicolay Draft</Italic>
          of the Gettysburg Address.
      </Inline>
```

```
</Block>
  ⋮
</TextPanel>
</Border>
```

Figure 3-8 shows the resulting output.

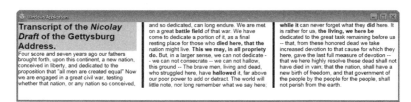

Figure 3-8   The *TextPanel* with multiple font characteristics, columns, and formatting

GridPanel

The *GridPanel* panel displays tabular data. The *GridPanel* supports many properties that you can use to customize the layout of the tabular data. For example, you can set the *Columns* and *Rows* properties to control the number of columns and rows in the grid. Similarly, the *ColumnStyles* and *RowStyles* properties allow you to set a collection of properties that the *GridPanel* applies to the rows and columns, respectively.

GridPanel arranges its children in order, starting with the upper left cell and moving to the right until the end of the row. A child can take more than one column if you set the *GridPanel.ColumnSpan* property on the child. Similarly, *GridPanel.RowSpan* allows a child to span multiple rows.

The following markup displays a Calculator user interface that looks quite similar to the Windows Calculator utility.

```
<Border xmlns="http://schemas.microsoft.com/2003/xaml" Background="#DEE7F7">
<DockPanel Dock="Left">
  <Border  BorderThickness="0,0,0,0">
<!-- Padding="10, 10, 10, 10"  -->
  <GridPanel Columns="7">
    <GridPanel.ColumnStyles>
      <Column Width="16%"/>
      <Column Width="4%"/>
      <Column Width="16%"/>
      <Column Width="16%"/>
      <Column Width="16%"/>
      <Column Width="16%"/>
      <Column Width="16%"/>
    </GridPanel.ColumnStyles>
```

```
<GridPanel.RowStyles>
  <Row Height="25"/>
  <Row Height="10"/>
  <Row Height="35"/>
  <Row Height="7"/>
  <Row Height="35"/>
  <Row Height="35"/>
  <Row Height="35"/>
  <Row Height="35"/>
</GridPanel.RowStyles>

    <Border GridPanel.ColumnSpan="7" BorderBrush="#DEE7F7"
            BorderThickness="2,2,2,2" Background="White">
      <Text HorizontalAlignment="right"
            ID="CalcText">0.</Text>
    </Border>

    <Text GridPanel.ColumnSpan="7"/>

    <Border BorderThickness="0,0,0,0">
      <GridPanel>
        <Border BorderBrush="#DEE7F7" BorderThickness="2,2,2,2">
          <Text Width="16%"
            HorizontalAlignment="center"></Text>
        </Border>
      </GridPanel>
    </Border>

    <Text Width="4%"/>
    <DockPanel GridPanel.ColumnSpan="5" Dock="Left">
      <Button Width="33.33%" Foreground="Red">Backspace</Button>
      <Button Width="33.33%" Foreground="Red">CE</Button>
      <Button Width="33.33%" Foreground="Red">C</Button>
    </DockPanel>

    <Text GridPanel.ColumnSpan="7"/>

    <Button Foreground="Red">MC</Button>
    <Text/>
    <Button Foreground="Blue">7</Button>
    <Button Foreground="Blue">8</Button>
    <Button Foreground="Blue">9</Button>
    <Button Foreground="Red">/</Button>
    <Button Foreground="Blue">sqrt</Button>

    <Button Foreground="Red">MR</Button>
    <Text/>
    <Button Foreground="Blue">4</Button>
```

```
            <Button Foreground="Blue">5</Button>
            <Button Foreground="Blue">6</Button>
            <Button Foreground="Red">*</Button>
            <Button Foreground="Blue">%</Button>

            <Button Foreground="Red">MS</Button>
            <Text/>
            <Button Foreground="Blue">1</Button>
            <Button Foreground="Blue">2</Button>
            <Button Foreground="Blue">3</Button>
            <Button Foreground="Red">-</Button>
            <Button Foreground="Blue">1/x</Button>

            <Button Foreground="Red">M+</Button>
            <Text/>
            <Button Foreground="Blue">0</Button>
            <Button Foreground="Blue">+/-</Button>
            <Button Foreground="Blue">.</Button>
            <Button Foreground="Red">+</Button>
            <Button Foreground="Red">=</Button>

        </GridPanel>
    </Border>
    </DockPanel>
</Border>
```

Figure 3-9 shows the resulting output.

Figure 3-9   The *GridPanel* as a calculator

FixedPanel

The *FixedPanel* panel allows you to specify the exact locations and sizes of every element. Elements on a *FixedPanel* will always display in the same location and size on all devices. I'll discuss the *FixedPanel* panel later in this chapter in the "Document Layout Services" section.

Controls

XAML has all the controls you've come to expect from Windows—buttons, check boxes, radio buttons, list boxes, combo boxes, menus, scroll bars, sliders, and so on. This sample demonstrates some of the common controls provided in Longhorn. You can see the results in Figure 3-10.

```
<Border
      xmlns="http://schemas.microsoft.com/2003/xaml"
      xmlns:def="Definition"
      Background="BlanchedAlmond"
   >
<DockPanel>
  <Menu DockPanel.Dock="Top">
    <MenuItem Header="File">
      <MenuItem Header="New" />
      <MenuItem Header="Open" />
    </MenuItem>

    <MenuItem Header="Edit">
      <MenuItem Header="Cut"/>
      <MenuItem Header="Copy"/>
      <MenuItem Header="Paste"/>
    </MenuItem>
  </Menu>

<FlowPanel>

<Button> Button </Button>
<Border Width="15"/>

<CheckBox Checked="true"> CheckBox </CheckBox>
<Border Width="15"/>

<RadioButtonList>
  <RadioButton> RadioButton 1 </RadioButton>
  <RadioButton Checked="true"> RadioButton 2 </RadioButton>
  <RadioButton> RadioButton 3 </RadioButton>
</RadioButtonList>
<Border Width="15"/>

<ListBox>
    <ListItem> ListItem 1 </ListItem>
```

```
      <ListItem> ListItem 2 </ListItem>
      <ListItem> ListItem 3 </ListItem>
   </ListBox>
   <Border Width="15"/>

   <ComboBox>
      <ListItem> ListItem 1 </ListItem>
      <ListItem> ListItem 2 </ListItem>
      <ListItem> ListItem 3 </ListItem>
   </ComboBox>
   <Border Width="15"/>

       <DockPanel>
         <VerticalSlider DockPanel.Dock="Top"  Height="200"
                 Minimum="0" Maximum="255" Value="75"
                 SmallChange="1" LargeChange="16"/>
         <Text DockPanel.Dock="Bottom">Slider</Text>
       </DockPanel>
   <Border Width="15"/>

       <DockPanel>
         <VerticalScrollBar DockPanel.Dock="Top"
                 Minimum="0" Maximum="255" Value="125" Height="200"
                 SmallChange="1" LargeChange="16"/>
         <Text DockPanel.Dock="bottom">ScrollBar</Text>
       </DockPanel>
   <Border Width="15"/>

   <TextBox> TextBox </TextBox>

   </FlowPanel>
   </DockPanel>
   </Border>
```

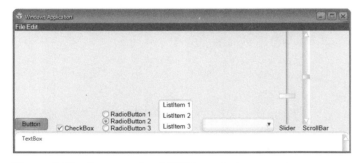

Figure 3-10 An example of XAML controls

XAML also allows you to combine elements and controls to create rich effects. We call this combining of elements *control composition*, and it is one of the most powerful aspects of Longhorn. For instance, to create a button with an image, you put an *Image* element inside *Button*:

```
<Button>
  <Image Source="tulip.jpg"/>
</Button>
```

To have both an image and text in the *Button*, as you can see in Figure 3-11, we use our old friend *DockPanel*:

```
<Button>
  <DockPanel>
    <Image Source="tulip.jpg"/>
    <Text DockPanel.Dock="fill" VerticalAlignment="center"> Button
      <Italic>with Image!</Italic>
    </Text>
  </DockPanel>
</Button>
```

Figure 3-11   A button with an image and text

You can put pretty much anything inside anything, including this strange example of a *CheckBox* inside a *Button*:

```
<Button>
  <CheckBox Checked="true"> CheckBox </CheckBox>
</Button>
```

Composition is powerful enough that many of the Longhorn controls are actually defined using composition. For instance, a *ScrollBar* is actually two buttons and a slider, plus some event handler logic to hook them together.

XAML also includes some control "primitives," which are primarily used with control composition to build larger effects. For instance, *ScrollViewer* takes one child (typically a panel) and adds scroll bars to it. This example places a very large list of *CheckBox* elements inside a *ScrollViewer*, something which prior to Longhorn required a separate control such as Windows Forms' *CheckedListBox*:

```
<Border BorderThickness="1" BorderBrush="black">
  <ScrollViewer Height="100" Width="200">
    <GridPanel Columns="1">
      <CheckBox Checked="true"> CheckBox 1</CheckBox>
      <CheckBox Checked="true"> CheckBox 2</CheckBox>
      <CheckBox Checked="true"> CheckBox 3</CheckBox>
      <CheckBox Checked="true"> CheckBox </CheckBox>
      <CheckBox Checked="true"> CheckBox </CheckBox>
      <CheckBox Checked="true"> CheckBox </CheckBox>
      <CheckBox Checked="true"> CheckBox </CheckBox>
      <CheckBox Checked="true"> CheckBox </CheckBox>
    </GridPanel>
  </ScrollViewer>
</Border>
```

Resources and Styles

XAML provides very rich facilities for customizing the look of your application, through entities known as styles. However, before we get into this topic, we need to learn about *resources*. The term *resources* used in this context simply refers to a way of reusing commonly defined objects and values. Let's look at an example:

```
<Border
      xmlns="http://schemas.microsoft.com/2003/xaml"
      xmlns:def="Definition"
      Background="BlanchedAlmond"
  >
  <FlowPanel>
    <FlowPanel.Resources>
      <SolidColorBrush def:Name="MyColor" Color="Gold"/>
    </FlowPanel.Resources>
    <Button Background="{MyColor}"/>
    <Ellipse Fill="{MyColor}"/>
  </FlowPanel>
</Border>
```

This code defines a new resource named *MyColor*, whose type is *Solid-ColorBrush* and value is *Gold*. This resource is part of the *FlowPanel*'s *Resources* collection. Every element has a *Resources* collection. You can define resources on any element you want, but most often you'll put them only on the root element—in this case, the *FlowPanel*.

Once you define a resource, you can then reference the resource in a property value by putting the resource name in braces, as you see here:

```
<Button Background="{MyColor}"/>
```

When the XAML processor sees *{MyColor}* in this example, it will first check the button's *Resources* collection. Because *Button* doesn't have a definition of *MyColor* (its *Resources* collection is empty), it will check the *Button*'s parent—the *FlowPanel*.

One particularly useful kind of resource is a *Style*. *Style* is both the name of class and the name of a property that all elements have. A *Style* defines properties to set on an element, which then uses that designated style. This example defines a *Style* called *MyStyle* and applies that style to a button:

```
<Border
      xmlns="http://schemas.microsoft.com/2003/xaml"
      xmlns:def="Definition"
      Background="BlanchedAlmond"
  >
  <FlowPanel>
    <FlowPanel.Resources>

      <Style def:Name="MyStyle">
          <Button Background="Red" FontSize="24"/>
      </Style>

    </FlowPanel.Resources>
    <Button>Normal</Button>

    <Button Style="{MyStyle}">Styled</Button>

  </FlowPanel>
</Border>
```

You can also define a *Style* resource with no name—which becomes the element's default style for elements where you do not specify an explicit *Style* property. This example adds a default style to the preceding example:

```
<Border
      xmlns="http://schemas.microsoft.com/2003/xaml"
      xmlns:def="Definition"
      Background="BlanchedAlmond"
  >
  <FlowPanel>
    <FlowPanel.Resources>

      <Style>
          <Button Background="Green" FontSize="15"/>
      </Style>
```

```
        <Style def:Name="MyStyle">
            <Button Background="Red" FontSize="24"/>
        </Style>
    </FlowPanel.Resources>
    <Button>Normal</Button>
    <Button Style="{MyStyle}">Styled</Button>
  </FlowPanel>
</Border>
```

You can do a kind of style inheritance by setting the *BasedOn* property of the *Style* class. Referencing the new *Style* class will set all the properties that the old *Style* did, plus the additional properties you specify. The following example defines two styles: the first sets the *Background* property, and the second, based on the first, sets the *FontSize* property.

```
<Border
        xmlns="http://schemas.microsoft.com/2003/xaml"
        xmlns:def="Definition"
        Background="BlanchedAlmond"
  >
  <FlowPanel>
    <FlowPanel.Resources>
      <Style def:Name="Style1">
          <Button Background="Red"/>
      </Style>

      <Style def:Name="Style2" BasedOn="{Style1}">
          <Button FontSize="24"/>
      </Style>
    </FlowPanel.Resources>
    <Button Style="{Style1}">Style 1</Button>
    <Button Style="{Style2}">Style 2</Button>
  </FlowPanel>
</Border>
```

It's even possible for a *Style* to set properties conditionally, using a feature known as *property triggers*. *Style* has a property named *VisualTriggers*, which is a collection of *PropertyTriggers*. Each *PropertyTrigger* specifies a condition using the *Property* and *Value* properties, and contains a collection of *Set* statements. When the styled element's property matches that value, the *Set* statements are applied, and when the condition is no longer true, the values are unapplied, as if they had never been set in the first place. This example uses property triggers to make the button green when the mouse is over the button, and red otherwise:

```
<Border
        xmlns="http://schemas.microsoft.com/2003/xaml"
            xmlns:def="Definition"
        Background="BlanchedAlmond"
  >
  <FlowPanel>
    <FlowPanel.Resources>
      <Style def:Name="Style1">
          <Button Background="Red"/>

          <Style.VisualTriggers>
            <PropertyTrigger Property="IsMouseOver" Value="true">
              <Set PropertyPath="Background" Value="Green"/>
            </PropertyTrigger>
            </Style.VisualTriggers>
      </Style>
    </FlowPanel.Resources>
    <Button Style="{Style1}">Style 1</Button>
  </FlowPanel>
</Border>
```

Many XAML controls use control composition. They combine a number of smaller controls to create a larger, more complicated control. Styles even let you change this! By specifying a different composition, you can completely redefine the look of a control while still keeping its behavior.

After you declare the style element and its properties, the *<Style.Visual-Tree>* tag specifies inside the *Style* which elements to compose to create the larger control. You can set child elements' properties as usual, and give to those children children of their own. You can also use property aliasing to set property values. For example, *Name1="*Alias(Target=Name2)"* will set the child's *Name1* property to the larger control's *Name2* property. The following example creates a style for *Button* that changes the composition to achieve a round look, as you can see in Figure 3-12. The button's *Background* and *Content* properties are aliased at appropriate points in the visual tree.

```
<Border Background="white"
    xmlns="http://schemas.microsoft.com/2003/xaml"
    xmlns:def="Definition">
  <FlowPanel>
    <FlowPanel.Resources>
      <Style def:Name="RoundButton">

        <Button FontSize="20"/>

        <Style.VisualTree>
```

```
    <Canvas>
        <Rectangle ID="MainRect"
            RadiusX="10" RadiusY="10"
            Fill="*Alias(Target=Background)"
            Width="100%" Height="100%" />

        <FlowPanel Width="100%" Height="100%" >
            <ContentPresenter
                ContentControl.Content="*Alias(Target = Content)"
                Margin="15,3,15,5"/>
        </FlowPanel>
    </Canvas>
  </Style.VisualTree>
</Style>
</FlowPanel.Resources>

<Button Style="{RoundButton}">
    standard RoundButton
</Button>

<Button Background="red" Style="{RoundButton}">
    red RoundButton
</Button>

<Button>
    standard button
</Button>

<Button Background="red">
    red standard button
</Button>
</FlowPanel>
</Border>
```

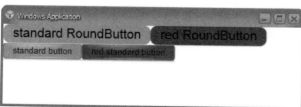

Figure 3-12   A couple of *RoundButton* and standard buttons on a *FlowPanel*

Graphics and Animations

XAML provides extensive support for drawing shapes, transforming the state of an object, and animating nearly any property of an object. You use *Shape* elements for drawing, *Transform* elements to altering a property or an object, and *Animation* elements to change a property of an object over time.

Shapes

XAML provides a set of *Shape* elements for drawing, which include *Ellipse*, *Line*, *Rectangle*, *Path*, *Polygon*, and *Polyline*. A *Shape* has a *Fill*, which is the background color, and a *Stroke*, which is the outline color. *Fill* and *Stroke* default to transparent, so make sure you set at least one of them! The *StrokeWidth* property controls the thickness of the outline.

Shapes can't have child elements. You typically place shapes inside a *Canvas*, so the first shape in markup will be the first one drawn. This example illustrates some of the basic shapes, which you can also see in Figure 3-13:

```
<Border
     xmlns="http://schemas.microsoft.com/2003/xaml"
     xmlns:def="Definition"
     Background="BlanchedAlmond"
  >
  <Canvas Height="400" Width="400">
      <Ellipse CenterX="70" CenterY="75"
       RadiusX="30" RadiusY="50"
       Fill="yellow" Stroke="red" StrokeThickness="15"/>

      <Rectangle RectangleLeft="150" RectangleTop="20"
       RectangleHeight="100" RectangleWidth="40"
       Fill="lightBlue" Stroke="green"/>

      <Line X1="20" Y1="220" X2="150" Y2="240"
       Stroke="black" StrokeThickness="5"/>

      <Polygon Points="220,140 270,240 170,240"
       StrokeLineJoin="Round"
       Stroke="black" StrokeThickness="20"/>
  </Canvas>
</Border>
```

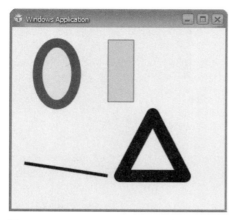

Figure 3-13 Various shapes on a *Canvas*

So far, we've used only solid colors with the *Stroke* and *Fill* properties. But in XAML, almost anywhere you can use a color you can specify a *Brush*. *Solid-ColorBrush* is the kind of brush we've been using so far, but XAML also supports *ImageBrush*, *LinearGradientBrush*, and *RadialGradientBrush*. *ImageBrush* has an *ImageSource* property that specifies the name of the image file. *SolidColor-Brush* has a *Color* property. *LinearGradientBrush* and *RadialGradientBrush* contain a *GradientStopCollection*, which allows for very complicated gradients. This example defines four brushes as resources, and uses them as the *Stroke* and *Fill* of the ellipses. You can see what they look like in Figure 3-14.

```
<Border
      xmlns="http://schemas.microsoft.com/2003/xaml"
      xmlns:def="Definition"
      Background="BlanchedAlmond"
  >
  <Border.Resources>
      <LinearGradientBrush def:Name="lineargradient" StartPoint="0,0"
                           EndPoint="1,1"  >
        <LinearGradientBrush.GradientStops>
          <GradientStopCollection>
            <GradientStop Color="Blue" Offset="0"/>
            <GradientStop Color="white" Offset="1"/>
          </GradientStopCollection>
        </LinearGradientBrush.GradientStops>
      </LinearGradientBrush>

      <RadialGradientBrush def:Name="radialgradient" Focus="0.3,0.3">
        <RadialGradientBrush.GradientStops>
```

```
      <GradientStopCollection>
        <GradientStop Color="red" Offset="0"/>
        <GradientStop Color="yellow" Offset="1"/>
      </GradientStopCollection>
    </RadialGradientBrush.GradientStops>
  </RadialGradientBrush>

  <ImageBrush def:Name="image" ImageSource="Tulip.jpg" TileMode="Tile"/>

  <SolidColorBrush def:Name="solid" Color="gray"/>
</Border.Resources>

<Canvas Height="400" Width="400">
    <Ellipse CenterX="100" CenterY="75"
     RadiusX="90" RadiusY="50"
     Fill="{lineargradient}" Stroke="{image}" StrokeThickness="15"/>

    <Ellipse CenterX="300" CenterY="170"
     RadiusX="50" RadiusY="150"
     Fill="{radialgradient}" Stroke="{solid}" StrokeThickness="15"/>
</Canvas>
</Border>
```

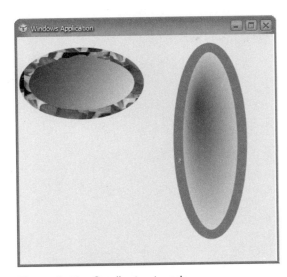

Figure 3-14   Gradients at work

Transforms

XAML supports several kinds of *Transforms*. *RotateTransform* rotates by the amount of the *Angle* property. *TranslateTransform* moves things according to the *X* and *Y* properties. *ScaleTransform* will shrink or stretch according to the *ScaleX* and *ScaleY* properties. *SkewTransform* slants things, using the *AngleX*, *AngleY*, and *Center* properties. *MatrixTransform* supports arbitrary affine transformations. Finally, *TransformCollection* is itself a *Transform* that allows you to combine several transforms together.

Some classes, such as *Brush*, have a *Transform* property. For other cases, you can use the *TransformDecorator* element, which has a *Transform* property. *TransformDecorator* will transform its child element. (Like *Border*, it can have only one child.) *TransformDecorator* can contain any kind of child, including shapes, panels, and controls. This example uses to *TransformDecorators*. The first contains an *Ellipse*, and rotates it 45 degrees. The second *TransformDecorator* contains a *ListBox* and both rotates and scales the *ListBox*. You can see what the shapes look like in Figure 3-15.

```
<Border
        xmlns="http://schemas.microsoft.com/2003/xaml"
        xmlns:def="Definition"
        Background="BlanchedAlmond"
  >
  <Canvas Height="400" Width="400">
    <TransformDecorator Transform="rotate 45">
      <Ellipse CenterX="100" CenterY="75"
        RadiusX="90" RadiusY="50"
        Fill="white" Stroke="black" StrokeThickness="15"/>
    </TransformDecorator>

    <TransformDecorator Canvas.Top="200" Canvas.Left="100">
      <TransformDecorator.Transform>
        <TransformCollection>
          <RotateTransform Angle="135"/>
          <ScaleTransform ScaleX="2" ScaleY="4"/>
        </TransformCollection>
      </TransformDecorator.Transform>

      <ListBox >
        <ListItem> ListItem 1 </ListItem>
        <ListItem> ListItem 2 </ListItem>
        <ListItem> ListItem 3 </ListItem>
      </ListBox>
    </TransformDecorator>
  </Canvas>
</Border>
```

Figure 3-15   A skewed *ListBox* and *Ellipse*

Animations

XAML also supports animations. You can animate nearly every property. Some properties have a corresponding "Animations" property—for example, *Rotate-Transform.Angle* and *RotateTransform.AngleAnimations*. In other cases, you can assign an *animation collection* to a property using compound property syntax. For example, see the following code:

```
<Button>
    <Button.Width>
      … put animation collection here …
    </Button.Width>
</Button>
```

Every type of property has a separate animations collection. The type of *Button.Width* is *Length*, so one uses the *LengthAnimationCollection*. Similarly, the *animation objects* themselves are specific to the type of the property you animate—the *LengthAnimationCollection* contains a set of *LengthAnimation* objects.

Animation objects have a *From* and *To* property, whose types match the type of the property being animated. The animation object also has *Begin*, *Duration*, and *End* properties, which are measured in seconds and control the timing of the animation. *Begin* also supports the value *Immediate*, and *Duration* supports *Indefinite*. You can use the *RepeatCount* and *RepeatDuration* properties to repeat the animation automatically. The *Fill* property specifies what happens to the property after the animation is over. *Fill="Hold"* is one of the most important values; it keeps the property at the animation *End* value.

Animation classes are not part of the default XAML namespace, so you will need to use the *<?Mapping>* and *xmlns* constructs to load the *MSAvalon.Windows.Media.Animation* namespace. Because this namespace contains classes from multiple DLLs, you'll need a separate *<?Mapping>* and *xmlns* for each DLL.

The next example animates two properties, the *RotateTransform.Angle* property and the *Button.Width* property, which use classes from both animation namespaces. Figure 3-16 shows the button at different times.

```
<?Mapping XmlNamespace="animC" ClrNamespace="MSAvalon.Windows.Media.Animation"
                               Assembly="PresentationCore" ?>
<?Mapping XmlNamespace="animF" ClrNamespace="MSAvalon.Windows.Media.Animation"
                               Assembly="PresentationFramework" ?>
<Border
      xmlns="http://schemas.microsoft.com/2003/xaml"
      xmlns:animC="animC"
      xmlns:animF="animF"
      xmlns:def="Definition"
      Background="BlanchedAlmond"
  >
  <Canvas Height="400" Width="400">
    <TransformDecorator Canvas.Top="200" Canvas.Left="100">
      <TransformDecorator.Transform>
        <TransformCollection>
          <RotateTransform Angle="135">
            <RotateTransform.AngleAnimations>
              <animC:DoubleAnimationCollection>
                <animC:DoubleAnimation From="0" To="360" Duration="4"
                  AutoReverse="True"
                  RepeatDuration="Indefinite"/>
              </animC:DoubleAnimationCollection>

            </RotateTransform.AngleAnimations>

          </RotateTransform>
        </TransformCollection>
      </TransformDecorator.Transform>

      <ListBox >
        <ListItem> ListItem 1 </ListItem>
        <ListItem> ListItem 2 </ListItem>
```

```
            <ListItem> ListItem 3 </ListItem>
          </ListBox>
      </TransformDecorator>

      <Button Width="40" Canvas.Top="10" Canvas.Left="10">
        <Button.Width>
          <animF:LengthAnimationCollection>
            <animF:LengthAnimation From="40" To="300"
              AutoReverse="true" Begin="1" Duration="1.2"
              RepeatDuration="Indefinite"/>
          </animF:LengthAnimationCollection>
        </Button.Width>
        Button
      </Button>

    </Canvas>
</Border>
```

Figure 3-16   Views of the animated button at different times

Document Services

The Longhorn platform provides extensive services that support a better online document viewing experience. There are two main services: a control designed for viewing, paginating, and navigating through the content of a document, and layout services designed to enhance the reading experience.

PageViewer Control

You use the PageViewer control when you want to display a document to the user for online viewing. The PageViewer control provides pagination and page navigation functionality. The control automatically formats the document's content into separate pages. The user can directly navigate to different pages using the controls provided by the page viewer.

Pagination and Navigation

Traditionally, online content, such as Web pages, was continuous. A user interface provided scroll bars to allow you to view content that couldn't fit in the visible area. In effect, you would "scroll" the view window to the position in the document you wished to see.

With pagination, you split the content of the document into one or more individual pages, similar to a book. The Longhorn platform provides support for paginated content by including several controls that help you display and navigate through content displayed as discrete pages. In addition, Longhorn provides a pagination application programming interface (API) to extend these capabilities and provide rich pagination support for custom pagination applications.

The PageViewer control is actually a complex control built from smaller controls using control composition techniques I've previously described. The PageViewer control uses the PageSource and the PageElement controls to provide its pagination functionality. The PageSource control breaks and formats the content across pages. The PageElement control renders a single page. The PageViewer control also uses the PageBar control to allow you to navigate through the pages.

Using the PageViewer control is very simple. To display a known document, you can use it as shown in the following code. Of course, you can hook up event handlers and change the source document to cause the page viewer to display different documents.

```
<Border
      xmlns="http://schemas.microsoft.com/2003/xaml"
      xmlns:def="Definition"
      Background="BlanchedAlmond"
   >
  <PageViewer Source="AuthorsandPublishers.xaml" />
</Border>
```

Figure 3-17 shows the page viewer hosted in a browser window displaying its document. Note the page navigation controls at the top of the document.

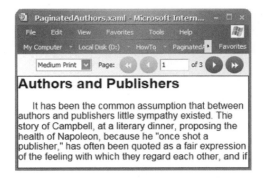

Figure 3-17   The PageViewer control

Document Layout Services

Longhorn also provides document layout services designed to make the reading experience better. Longhorn contains support for two new types of documents:

- Adaptive flow documents
- Fixed layout documents

These new document formats allow developers to provide their applications' users a better document reading experience.

Adaptive flow documents use specialized markup elements that declare that a document should be Adaptive. Longhorn automatically optimizes an adaptive document to best use the available screen space and provide the best reading experience for the user based on the capabilities or limitations of his or her system.

For example, the user might have one of the recently introduced 16-by-9 aspect ratio wide-screen displays. It's very difficult to read a line of text that spans a lengthy horizontal line. Depending on the width of the window, an adaptive document might divide the text into two, three, or more columns, thus reducing the effort for a user to scan a text line.

In another example, a document might contain an image and text that flows around the image. As you shrink the size of the document's window in a nonadaptive document, the image remains a fixed size and you see less and less of the text. An adaptive document could shrink the image when it determines that insufficient text is visible in the window. This allows the reader to still get a general idea of what the image portrays but continue to read the text in the context of the image. In a smaller window, seeing every pixel of an image is likely to be less important and useful to the reader than being able to read more text. An alternative, such as separating the image and surrounding text onto separate pages, defeats the intent of the document's author, which was to present the text and image together in context.

Fixed layout documents appear the same every time, regardless of the viewer's screen size, window size, or output device. You create a fixed layout document using specialized markup elements or by printing a document using a Microsoft Windows Vector Graphics (WVG) printer driver.

Adaptive Layout Documents

In an adaptive layout document, you supply key preferences in the root-level markup. Longhorn then can render the document in a way that makes best use of the window area and enhances its readability. Longhorn automatically determines the optimum width and number of columns for a page, ideal sizes for all text elements, optimum sizes and positions for all figures, and the widths of margins and gutters to give the best overall presentation of the content.

Producing an Adaptive Layout Document

To create an adaptive layout document, use declarative markup similar to the following:

```
<Border
      xmlns="http://schemas.microsoft.com/2003/xaml"
      xmlns:def="Definition"
      Background="BlanchedAlmond"
  >
  <AdaptiveMetricsContext ColumnPreference="Medium"
                          FontFamily="Arial">
    <TextPanel Background="white">
      <Section>
        <Heading OutlineLevel="1">Adaptive Layout Example</Heading>
        <Paragraph>
This example shows the advanced capabilities of Adaptive Flow Layout. Lorem ips
um dolor sit  amet, consectetuer adipiscing elit, sed diam nonummy nibh euismod
 tincidunt ut laoreet  dolore magna aliquam erat volutpat. Ut wisi enim ad mini
m veniam, quis nostrud exerci tation  ullamcorper suscipit lobortis nisl ut ali
quip ex ea commodo consequat. Duis autem vel eum  iriure.</Paragraph>
        <Paragraph>
        <Image TextPanel.FlowBehavior="Figure" Source="picture1.jpg"
            TextPanel.Emphasis="Medium" />
Notice how images and text are flowed intelligently to enhance the reading expe
rience. Lorem  ipsum dolor sit amet, consectetuer adipiscing elit, sed diam non
ummy nibh euismod tincidunt  ut laoreet dolore magna aliquam erat volutpat. Ut
wisi enim ad minim veniam, quis nostrud  exerci tation ullamcorper suscipit lob
ortis nisl ut aliquip ex ea commodo consequat. Duis  autem vel eum iriure.
</Paragraph>
```

```
    <Paragraph>Adaptive layout is an exciting new feature of Longhorn.
    <Image TextPanel.FlowBehavior="Figure" Source="picture2.jpg"
         TextPanel.Emphasis="Low" />
Lorem ipsum dolor sit amet, consectetuer adipiscing elit, sed diam nonummy nibh
euismod  tincidunt ut laoreet dolore magna aliquam erat volutpat. Ut wisi enim
ad minim veniam, quis  nostrud exerci tation ullamcorper suscipit lobortis nis
l ut aliquip ex ea commodo consequat.  Duis autem vel eum xriure.</Paragraph>
      </Section>
    </TextPanel>
  </AdaptiveMetricsContext>
</Border>
```

Fixed-Layout Documents

You use a fixed-layout document to present the document contents in exactly the same layout and format, independent of the application software, hardware, and operating system used. In addition, a fixed-layout document renders identically on all output devices. A fixed-layout document is a set of objects that collectively describe the appearance of one or more pages.

Producing a Fixed-Layout Document

You can use two different techniques to produce a fixed-layout document:

- Print a document without markup to a file using the Longhorn printer driver

- Write a fixed-layout document using XAML

When you print a document using most Microsoft Win32 applications (for example, Microsoft Office) using the Longhorn printer driver, the printer driver will create an XAML file that contains markup to paginate and position each character, image, or vector graphic in the printed document.

You can choose to output the document as a markup file directly or to include the markup file inside a container. When you select container output, you can also apply digital rights and document protection to the document.

Alternatively, you can create XAML using an editor. The following is a skeletal example of fixed-layout document:

```
<FixedPanel xmlns="http://schemas.microsoft.com/2003/xaml/" >
  <FixedPage Width="8.50in" Height="11.00in"> <!-- PAGE 1 -->
    <Text FontFamily="Arial" FontSize="8.4" FixedPage.Left="1.250in"
         FixedPage.Top="0.530in" FontWeight="Bold">1.</Text>
    <Text FontFamily="Arial" FixedPage.Left="1.350in" FixedPage.Top="0.500in"
         FontWeight="Bold" FontSize="12">Fixed Document</Text>
  </FixedPage>
```

```
<FixedPage>
  <Text>This is page 2</Text>
</FixedPage>
<FixedPage>
  <Text>This is page 3</Text>
</FixedPage>
</FixedPanel>
```

Summary

Panels allow you to divide the display surface into areas with different layout characteristics. You have a great variety of controls that you can use to populate the panels of a display. *Shapes*, *Transforms*, and *Animations* allow you to produce dynamic graphical output. Using control composition, you can combine these features to produce practically any user interface you want. You can produce adaptive documents that lay out your content intelligently and make it easy for the reader to read. Alternatively, you can precisely position every single element on a page and control pagination explicitly to produce a document that appears exactly as you want regardless of the output device. What's more, you can do it all declaratively using XAML. This sure as heck beats writing a WM_PAINT message handler!

4

Storage

In some ways, *personal computer* is an inadequate name. Most people don't use a personal computer to compute. They use a computer to communicate (through e-mail or instant messaging) and to store and organize their personal data (such as e-mail, documents, pictures, and digital music). Unfortunately, while your computer presently stores this data quite well, it does a relatively poor job of allowing you to organize the information so that you can find it later.

Disk capacity has been growing at roughly 70 percent annually over the last decade. It's presently possible to buy drives with more than 250 gigabytes (GB) of storage. It's likely that 500-GB drives will become available in the next few years and that many systems will have more than one disk drive. I just did a quick check on the computer on which I'm writing this chapter, and I have 283,667 files in 114,129 folders in only 200 GB of disk space. When I forget exactly where I put a file, it can take quite a while to find it again. In the worst case, I have to search the entire contents of each disk. In a few years, people will be able to store millions of files, most of which, if nothing improves, they'll never see again.

One reason people have difficulty finding information on their computer is because of the limited ability for the user to organize data. The present file system support for folders and files worked well originally because it was a familiar paradigm to most people and the number of files was relatively small. However, it doesn't easily allow you to store an image of your coworker Bob playing softball at the 2007 company picnic at a local park and later find the image when searching for documents that

- Mention Bob
- Involve sports

- Relate to company events

- Pertain to the park or its surrounding area

- Were created in 2007

The hierarchical folder structure doesn't work well when you want to categorize data in numerous ways. Therefore, we have a problem today in that we have lots of stuff to store and no good way to categorize it. In addition to categorizing information, which many people associate with attaching a fixed set of keywords to data, people need to relate data. For example, I might want to relate a picture to the company picnic, or I might want to relate a picture to Bob, who is also a member of an organization to which I donate time and effort, as a contact.

Another problem is that we store the same stuff in multiple places in multiple formats. Developers spend much time and effort creating their own, unique storage abstractions for everyday information such as People, Places, Times, and Events. For example, Microsoft Outlook has a definition of a Contact. The Microsoft Windows Address Book also has its own definition of a contact. Each instant messaging application has yet another. Each application stores its definition of a contact in a unique, isolated silo of information.

There are a number of problems with current approaches to data storage, including the following:

- Developers reinvent the basic data abstractions repeatedly.

- Multiple applications cannot easily share common data.

- The same information lives in multiple locations.

- The user repeatedly enters the same information.

- Separate copies of data become unsynchronized.

- There are no notifications of data change.

What Is WinFS?

WinFS is the new storage system in Longhorn. It improves the Microsoft Windows platform in three ways. First, it allows you to categorize your information in multiple ways and relate one item of information to another. Second, it provides a common storage format for information collected on an everyday basis, such as information dealing with people, places, images, and more. Third, it promotes data sharing of common information across multiple applications from multiple vendors.

WinFS Is a Storage Platform

WinFS is an active storage platform for organizing, searching for, and sharing all kinds of information. This platform defines a rich data model that allows you to use and define rich data types that the storage platform can use. WinFS contains numerous schemas that describe real entities such as Images, Documents, People, Places, Events, Tasks, and Messages. These entities can be quite complex. For example, a person can have multiple names, multiple physical and e-mail addresses, a current location, and much more.

Independent software vendors (ISVs) can also define their own new data types and provide their schema to WinFS. By allowing WinFS to manage complex storage problems, an ISV can concentrate on developing its unique application logic and leverage the richer storage facilities of WinFS for its everyday and custom data.

WinFS contains a relational engine that allows you to locate instances of storage types by using powerful, relational queries. WinFS allows you to combine these storage entities in meaningful ways using relationships. One contact can be a member of the Employee group of an Organization while concurrently a member of the Household group for a specific address. ISVs automatically gain the ability to search, replicate, secure, and establish relationships among their unique data types as well as among the predefined Windows data types.

This structure allows the user to pose questions to the system and ask it to locate information rather than asking the system to individually search folders. For example, you can ask WinFS to find all e-mail messages from people on your instant messenger buddy list for which you don't have a phone number. Using relational queries, you can find all members of a Household for a particular employee with a birthday in the current month.

WinFS also supports multiple flexible programming models that allow you to choose the appropriate application programming interface (API) for the task. You can access the store by using traditional relational queries using structured query language (SQL). Alternatively, you can use .NET classes and objects to access the data store. You can also use XML-based APIs on the data store. WinFS also supports data access through the traditional Microsoft Win32 file system API. You can even mix and match—that is, use multiple APIs for a single task. However, for most purposes, developers will use the managed class APIs to change data in the WinFS store. It will often be far more complex to make an update using raw SQL statements as compared to using the object APIs.

In addition, WinFS provides a set of data services for monitoring, managing, and manipulating your data. You can register to receive events when particular data items change. You can schedule WinFS to replicate your data to other systems.

WinFS Is a File System

For traditional file-based data, such as text documents, audio tracks, and video clips, WinFS is the new Windows file system. Typically, you will store the main data of a file, the file stream, as a file on an NTFS volume. However, whenever you call an API that changes or adds items with NTFS file stream parts, WinFS extracts the metadata from the stream and adds the metadata to the WinFS store. This metadata describes information about the stream, such as its path, plus any information that WinFS can extract from the stream. Depending on file contents, this metadata can be the author (of a document), the genre (of an audio file), keywords (from a PDF file), and more. WinFS synchronizes the NTFS-resident file stream and the WinFS-resident metadata. New Longhorn applications can also choose to store their file streams directly in WinFS. File streams can be accessed using the existing Win32 file system API or the new WinFS API.

WinFS Isn't Just a File System

A file system manages files and folders. While WinFS does manage files and folders, it also manages all types of nonfile-based data, such as personal contacts, event calendars, tasks, and e-mail messages. WinFS data can be structured, semistructured, or unstructured. Structured data includes a schema that additionally defines what the data is for and how you should use it. Because WinFS is, in part, a relational system, it enforces data integrity with respect to semantics, transactions, and constraints.

WinFS isn't just a relational system, either. It supports both hierarchical storage and relational storage. It supports returning data as structured types and as objects—types plus behavior. You might consider WinFS a hierarchical, relational, object-oriented data storage system—although it actually contains certain aspects of each of those traditional storage systems. WinFS extends beyond the traditional file system and relational database system. It is the store for all types of data on the newest Windows platform.

WinFS and NTFS

You can store a file either in the traditional NTFS file system or in the new WinFS data store just like you can store things in FAT32 or on CD-ROMs or in NTFS today. Normally, a file stored in NTFS is not visible in WinFS. Longhorn applications using the new WinFS APIs can access data stored either in WinFS or in NTFS. In addition, Longhorn applications can continue to use the Win32 API to access data stored in the NTFS file system.

File Promotion

Files are either in WinFS or not. Any item that has a file stream part can participate in promotion/demotion, which we more generally call *metadata handling*. When WinFS promotes a file, it extracts the metadata from the known NTFS file content and adds the metadata to the WinFS data store. The actual data stream of the file remains in the NTFS file system. You can then query WinFS regarding the metadata as if the file natively resides within WinFS. WinFS also detects changes in the NTFS file and updates the metadata within the WinFS data store as necessary.

File Import and Export

You can also import a file to WinFS from NTFS and export a file from WinFS to NTFS. Importing and exporting a file moves both the file content and the metadata. After importing or exporting, the new file is completely independent of the original file.

WinFS Programming Model

The WinFS programming model includes data access, data manipulation, WinFS data class extensibility, data synchronization, data change notifications, and event prioritization. Data access and data manipulation allow you to create, retrieve, update, and delete data stored within WinFS and to exercise domain-specific behaviors. Data class extensibility enables you to extend WinFS schemas with custom fields and custom types. Data synchronization allows you to synchronize data between WinFS stores and between a WinFS and a non-WinFS store.

The top of the WinFS data model hierarchy is a WinFS *service*, which is simply an instance of WinFS. One level in the hierarchy from the service is a *volume*. A volume is the largest autonomous container of items. Each WinFS instance contains one or more volumes. Within a volume are *items*.

WinFS introduces the item as the new unit of consistency and operation, rather than the file. The storage system stores items. You have rich query ability over items. An item is effectively a base type of the storage system. An item therefore has a set of data attributes and provides a basic query capability.

People typically organize data in the real world according to some system that makes sense in a given domain. All such systems partition data into named groups. WinFS models this notion with the concept of a *folder*. A folder is a special type of item. There are two types of folders: *containment folders* and *virtual folders*.

A containment folder is an item that contains holding links to other items and models the common concept of a file system folder. An item exists as long as at least one holding link references it. Note that a containment folder doesn't directly contain the items logically present in the folder but instead contains links to those items. This allows multiple containment folders to *contain* the same item.

A virtual folder is a dynamic collection of items. It is a named set of items. You can either enumerate the set explicitly or specify a query that returns the members of the set. A virtual folder specified by a query is quite interesting. When you add a new item to the store that meets the criteria of the query for a virtual folder, the new item is automatically a member of the virtual folder. A virtual folder is itself an item. Conceptually, it represents a set of nonholding links to items, as you can see in Figure 4-1.

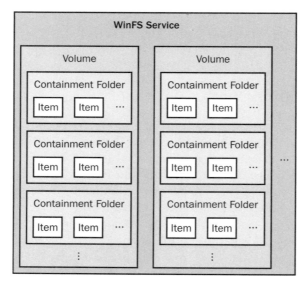

Figure 4-1   The WinFS data model hierarchy

Sometimes, you need to model a highly constrained notion of containment—for example, a Microsoft Word document embedded in an e-mail message is, in a sense, bound more tightly to its container than, for example, a file contained within a folder. WinFS expresses this notion by using *embedded items*. An embedded item is a special kind of link within an item (named Embedded Link) that references another item. The referenced item can be bound to or otherwise manipulated only within the context of the containing item.

Finally, WinFS provides the notion of *categories* as a way to classify items. You can associate one or more categories with every item in WinFS. WinFS, in effect, tags the category name onto the item. You can then specify the category name in searches. The WinFS data model allows the definition of a hierarchy of categories, thus enabling a tree-like classification of data.

Organizing Information

All these features together allow five ways to organize your information in WinFS:

- **Hierarchical folder-based organization**   With this approach, you still have the traditional hierarchical folder and item organization structure. All items in a WinFS data store must reside in a container, and one of these container types is a folder.

- **Type-based organization**   An item is always of a particular type. For example, you have Person items, Photo items, Organization items, and many other available types. You can even create new types and store them in the WinFS data store.

- **Item property–based organization**   You can view items that have one or more properties set to specified values. This is, in effect, a virtual folder view with a query that returns the items with the specified value for the specified properties.

- **Relationship-based organization**   You can retrieve items based on their relationship to other items—for example, a Person can be a member of an Organization, and either one can be organized or searched for in terms of this relationship.

- **Category-based organization**   You can create and associate any number of user-defined keywords with an item. Subsequently you can retrieve the items that have a specific value for an associated keyword. You won't, however, be able to create categorization taxonomies, so this organization technique is not as powerful as the preceding approaches.

WinFS APIs

WinFS provides three data access APIs: the managed WinFS API, the ADO.NET API, and the Win32 API. The WinFS API is a strongly typed "high level" API. ADO.NET provides a lower level API for working with data as XML or as tables or rows. Using ADO.NET, you can access data stored in WinFS by using Transact-Structured Query Language (T-SQL) and, when you want, retrieve data in XML using the T-SQL's FOR XML capability. The Win32 API allows access to the files and folders stored in WinFS.

You might prefer to use multiple access patterns to solve a problem. For example, you can issue a T-SQL query that returns a set of contacts as managed objects of the WinFS Contact type. Regardless of the API you use, each API ultimately manipulates data in the WinFS store using T-SQL.

In many cases, you will prefer to use the managed WinFS API. These .NET Framework classes automatically perform the object-relationship mapping needed to translate between object-oriented programming constructs, and they perform the necessary T-SQL to achieve the WinFS data access.

Using the Managed WinFS Classes

The WinFS managed classes reside in the *System.Storage* namespace and its nested namespaces. Many applications will also use WinFS type definitions from the *System.Storage.Core* namespace. You can additionally use types from more specialized namespaces. For example, the managed classes that manipulate the system definition of a Contact reside in the *System.Storage.Contact* namespace. For simplicity, all the code examples in this chapter will use the following set of *using* declarations:

```
using System.Storage;
using System.Storage.Core;
using System.Storage.Contact;
```

ItemContext

The WinFS store consists of items organized into folders and categorized. The first step in working with WinFS is to identify the set of items with which you want to work. We call this process *binding*, and the set of items can be any of the following:

- An entire volume (also known as the *root folder*)

- An identifiable subset of items in a given volume—for example, a particular containment folder or virtual folder

- An individual item

- A WinFS share (which identifies a volume, a folder, a virtual folder, or an individual item)

To bind to a set of items, you create a *System.Storage.ItemContext* object and connect it to a WinFS data store. Use the static *System.Storage.ItemContext.Open* helper method to create an *ItemContext* object.

The following code creates an *ItemContext* that connects to the default local WinFS volume. The default is the *local-computer-name*\DefaultStore share:

```
System.Storage.ItemContext ctx = System.Storage.ItemContext.Open ();
⋮
ctx.Close();
```

Alternatively, you can pass a string to the constructor to connect the item context to a specific WinFS store. The following code creates an item context connected to a WinFS share identified by the \\machine\Legal Documents share:

```
ItemContext ctx = null;
try {
ctx = ItemContext.Open (@"\machine\Legal Documents");
  ⋮
}
finally {
  if (ctx != null) ctx.Dispose();
}
```

Be sure to close or dispose of the context object as soon as you finish using it regardless of exceptions. An *ItemContext* uses significant unmanaged resources—such as a connection to the store—that you should free up in a timely manner. To make closing contexts as convenient as possible, the *ItemContext* class implements the *IDisposable* interface. Therefore, you can use the C# *using* statement as shown in the following example to release these resources:

```
using (ItemContext ctx = ItemContext.Open (@"D:\MyStore")) {
⋮
}
```

Storing a New Item in a WinFS Data Store

Every item in a WinFS data store must be a member of a folder of the store. You obtain the root of the folder hierarchy by calling the extremely well-named static method *System.Storage.Folder.GetRootFolder*. However, there are also several system-defined containers for storing application-specific data. You often use one of the static methods on the *UserDataFolder* class to retrieve a folder in which you then place new items.

Getting a Folder

In the following example, I'll find the current user's Personal Contacts folder if it exists and create it when it doesn't exist. Note that this is a somewhat contrived example—the system automatically creates a user's Personal Contacts folder if it doesn't exist when the user first logs into a system—but it gives me a chance to show how to create an expected folder when it doesn't exist.

```
ItemContext ctx = ItemContext.Open ();
WellKnownFolder contactsFolder =
        UserDataFolder.FindUsersWellKnownFolderWithType (ctx,
                        GeneralCategories.PersonalContactsFolder);

if (contactsFolder == null) {
    //create the Personal Contacts folder
    Folder userDataFolder = UserDataFolder.FindMyUserDataFolder (ctx);
    WellKnownFolder subFolder = new WellKnownFolder (ctx);
    CategoryRef category = new CategoryRef (ctx,
                        GeneralCategories.PersonalContactsFolder);

    // Associate the PersonalContactsFolder category to the folder
    subFolder.FolderType = category;
    userDataFolder.AddMember (subFolder);
    ctx.Update();
}
```

The preceding code does a number of interesting things. First, I try to locate an existing folder contained in the user's personal data folder hierarchy. I'm not looking for the folder by a well-known name. Instead, I'm locating the folder within the user's personal data tree that has previously been associated with the well-known category *PersonalContactsFolder*. The shell displays this folder when you select My Contacts.

This folder normally already exists, but when it doesn't, I retrieve the root folder for the user's data hierarchy. I create a new item, of type *WellKnown-Folder*, and then create a reference to a well-known category—the *Personal-ContactsFolder* category. I then set the type of the new folder to the *PersonalContactsFolder* category type, and finally, I add the new folder to its containing folder—the user's personal data root folder. WinFS doesn't save any changes to the data store until you call *Update* on the item context (which I regularly forget to do).

Of course, this is the verbose way to find the Personal Contacts folder. I wanted to show you how things work. Normally, I'd use the following code instead. The *FindMyPersonalContactsFolder* method finds the existing folder.

```
WellKnownFolder userDataFolder =
        UserDataFolder.FindMyPersonalContactsFolder (ctx);
```

Creating a New Item

As I now have the Personal Contacts folder, it seems appropriate to create a new contact in the folder. In the following example, I'll create a number of Person contacts and add them to the folder:

```
Person[] CreateFriends (ItemContext ctx) {
  string[] GivenNames = { "Monica", "Rachel", "Chandler",
                          "Joey",   "Phoebe", "Ross"};
  string[] SurNames = { "Uchra",     "Emerald",  "Ranier",
                        "Fibonacci", "Smorgasbord", "Uchra"};
  Person[] Friends = new Person [GivenNames.Length];

  for (int index = 0; index < GivenNames.Length; index++) {
    string linkName = GivenNames[index] + " " + SurNames[index];
    Person p = Person.CreatePersonalContact (ctx, linkName);
    Friends[index] = p;

    p.DisplayName = linkName;
    FullName fn = p.GetPrimaryName ();
    fn.GivenName = GivenNames[index];
    fn.Surname = SurNames[index];
  }
  ctx.Update ();
}
```

The prior code uses the static *Person.CreatePersonalContact* method. This method

- Creates a new Person item in the specified item context

- Creates a new *FolderMember* relationship with the specified name that references the Person

- Adds the *FolderMember* relationship to the *PersonalContactsFolder*'s *Relationship* collection

I subsequently update the *DisplayName, GivenName*, and *Surname* properties of the Person item. As always, I call *Update* on the item context to save the changes to the data store.

Let's look more closely at the *CreatePersonalContact* method. It is equivalent to the following:

```
// Find the PersonalContacts folder
WellKnownFolder contactsFolder =
        UserDataFolder.FindUsersWellKnownFolderWithType (ctx,
                          GeneralCategories.PersonalContactsFolder);
// Create a new Person item
Person p = new Person (ctx);

// Need a folder relationship that references the new Person
FolderMember fm = new FolderMember (p, linkName);
folder.Relationships.Add (fm);
ctx.Update ();
```

Relationship Items

WinFS defines a relationship data model that allows you to relate items to one another. When you define the schema for a data type, you can define zero or more relationships as part of the schema. For example, the Folder schema defines the *FolderMember* relationship. The Organization schema defines the *Employee* relationship. For each such defined relationship, there is a class that represents the relationship itself. This class is derived from the *Relationship* class and contains members specific to the relationship type. There is also a strongly typed "virtual" collection class. This class is derived from *VirtualRelationshipCollection* and allows relationship instances to be created and deleted.

A relationship relates a source item to a target item. In the previous example, the Personal Contacts folder was the source item and the Person item was the target item. The *FolderMember* relationship basically indicates that the Person item relates to the Personal Contacts folder as a member of the folder.

When you define a relationship, you define whether the relationship keeps the target item in existence—a *holding relationship*—or doesn't keep the target item in existence—a *reference relationship*. When you create a holding relationship to a target item, WinFS increments a reference count on the target item. When WinFS deletes a holding relationship it decrements the reference count on the target item. An item no longer exists in the store when its reference count reaches zero. WinFS never alters the reference count of the target when you create or destroy a reference relationship to the target. Therefore, the target item can disappear from the store when its reference count reaches zero and the relationship might refer to a no-longer-existing item.

WinFS defines the *FolderMember* relationship as a holding relationship. Most other relationship classes are reference relationships.

Folder Items

Now that you know about Link items, I can refine my description of Folder items. A Folder is a WinFS item that has a collection of Link items. The target of each Link item in the collection is a member of the folder. The *Folder.Members* property represents this collection of links.

Note this gives a WinFS folder much greater flexibility than traditional file system folders. The members of a folder can be file and nonfile items. Multiple links to a particular item can reside in many folders concurrently. In other words, multiple folders can *contain* the same item.

Other Item Types

Generally, you create other item types in the WinFS store as you did in the previous examples. Each type occasionally has its own special usage pattern. For example, we can have organizations as members of our Personal Contacts folder, so let's create one:

```
Organization cp = FindOrCreateOrganization (ctx, "Main Benefit");
⋮
Organization FindOrCreateOrganization (ItemContext ctx, string orgName) {
  Organization o =
    Organization.FindOne (ctx, "DisplayName='" + orgName + "'");
  if (o == null) {
    Folder Pcf = UserDataFolder.FindMyPersonalContactsFolder (ctx);

    o = new Organization (ctx);
    o.DisplayName = orgName;

    Folder pcf = UserDataFolder.FindMyPersonalContactsFolder (ctx);

    pcf.AddMember (o, o.DisplayName.ToString ());
    ctx.Update ();
  }
  return o;
}
```

Now let's add an employee to that organization:

```
enum Names { Monica, Rachel, Chandler, Joey, Phoebe, Ross }
⋮
Person[] Friends = CreateFriends (ctx);
Organization cp = FindOrCreateOrganization (ctx, "Main Benefit");
AddEmployeeToOrganization (ctx, Friends [(int)Names.Rachel],
  cp);
⋮
void AddEmployeeToOrganization (ItemContext ctx, Person p, Organization o) {
  EmployeeData ed = new EmployeeData (ctx);

  ed.Name = p.DisplayName;
  ed.Target_Key = p.ItemID_Key;
  o.Employees.Add (ed);
  ctx.Update ();
}
```

Similarly, we can create households in our Personal Contacts folders. Note that a household doesn't imply a family. A household might be a group of roommates. WinFS has additional schema for families, but I'll leave that as an exercise for the reader.

```
CreateHousehold (ctx, Friends [(int) Names.Chandler],
                      Friends [(int) Names.Joey]);
CreateHousehold (ctx, Friends [(int) Names.Monica],
                      Friends [(int) Names.Rachel]);
⋮
```

```
void CreateHousehold (ItemContext ctx, Person p1, Person p2) {
    Household h = new Household (ctx);
    h.DisplayName = p1.GetPrimaryName().GivenName + " and " +
                    p2.GetPrimaryName().GivenName + " household";

    Folder pcf = UserDataFolder.FindMyPersonalContactsFolder (ctx);
    pcf.AddMember (h, h.DisplayName.ToString ());

    // Add first person to the household
    HouseholdMemberData hhmd = new HouseholdMemberData (ctx);
    hhmd.Name = p1.DisplayName;
    hhmd.Target_Key = p1.ItemID_Key;
    h.HouseholdMembers.Add (hhmd);

    // Add second person to the household
    hhmd = new HouseholdMemberData (ctx);
    hhmd.Name = p2.DisplayName;
    hhmd.Target_Key = p2.ItemID_Key;
    h.HouseholdMembers.Add (hhmd);
}
```

The prior example uses one concept I've not yet discussed. Note the use of the *ItemID_Key* property in this line of code:

```
hhmd.Target_Key = p1.ItemID_Key;
```

Basically, the *ItemID_Key* value is another way to reference an item in the WinFS store, so let's look at the ways to find items in the store.

How to Find Items

Of course, it doesn't do much good to place items in a data store if you cannot subsequently find them easily. The *ItemContext* class contains instance methods you can use to retrieve items in a WinFS data store. You specify what type of item to find and any special constraints that the returned items must meet. In addition, each item class—for example, *Person*, *File*, *Folder*, and so forth—also contains static methods that allow you to find items of that particular type.

The *FindAll* method returns one or more items that match the specified criteria. The *ItemContext.FindAll* instance method requires you to specify the type of the items to locate. In addition, you can optionally specify search criteria to narrow the scope of search. For example, the following code finds all the Person items that have a *DisplayName* property whose value begins with "Brent".

```
FindResult res = ctx.FindAll (typeof(Person), "DisplayName='Brent%'");
foreach (Person p in res) {
    // Use the Person item somehow
}
```

Alternatively, I could use the static *FindAll* method of the *Person* class like this:

```
FindResult res = Person.FindAll (ctx, "DisplayName='Brent%'");
foreach (Person p in res) {
    // Use the Person item somehow
}
```

In both of these examples, the *FindAll* method always returns a collection of the items matching the type and specified criteria. This collection might contain no items, but you don't receive a null reference for the *FindResult*. Therefore, always iterate over the collection to obtain the items found.

When you know that only a single item will match the type requested and specified filter criteria, you can use the *FindOne* method. Be careful, however—the *FindOne* method throws an exception when it finds more than one item that matches your request.

```
Person p = Person.FindOne (ctx, "DisplayName='Brent Rector'");
```

The second string parameter is a filter expression that allows you to specify additional constraints the returned items must satisfy. The basic format of the filter expression is a string in the form "*<propertyName> <operator> <propertyValue>*".

WinFS calls the expression an *OPath* expression. The syntax is similar, although not identical, to the *XPath* expression syntax used for identifying items in an XML document. This code fragment returns all File items for files with either a "doc" or a "txt" file extension:

```
FindResult Files = File.FindAll (ctx, "Extension='doc' || Extension='txt'");
```

These expressions can be quite complex. For example, the following statement returns all Person items that represent employees of an employer with the *DisplayName* of "Main Benefit":

```
string pattern = "Source(EmployeeOf).DisplayName='Main Benefit'";
FindResult result = Person.FindAll (ctx, pattern);
```

Here's another one. I want the Person items where the Surname is not "Ranier" and the e-mail addresses don't end with ".edu".

```
string filter = "PersonalNames[Surname!='Ranier'] &&
                !(PersonalEmailAddresses[Address like '%.edu'])");
FindResult result = Person.FindAll (ctx, filter);
```

Identifying a Specific Item

You frequently need to create references to items in the WinFS store. Eventually, you use these references to locate the appropriate item. Earlier in this chapter, I showed you how to use a link to reference an item. Links use a friendly string-based identity for the reference, and this string name must be unique within the link's containing folder. In other words, you need both the folder and one of its contained links to identify the referenced item.

However, you can create multiple links with the same friendly string name as long as you add the links to different folders so that all names within a single folder remain unique. Note that these multiple links with the same friendly text name don't actually have to reference the same target item. They could, but they don't have to.

In such cases, searching for all links with a specific friendly text name (using *FindAll*, for example) will return multiple results. You will then need to examine the source of each link to determine the containing folder, and then determine which link references the desired item.

We need a way to reference any arbitrary item in the store—for example, suppose I want the 3,287th item in the store. Fortunately, you can do exactly this.

Finding an Item by *ItemID_Key* Value

WinFS assigns each newly created item a GUID-based identification number, known as its *ItemID_Key* property. In practice, an *ItemID_Key* value is highly likely to be unique across all WinFS volumes; however, WinFS still treats this identifier as if it's unique only within a volume. You can use this volume unique value to identify any item in a WinFS volume.

```
Item GetItem (ItemContext ctx, SqlBinary itemID_Key) {
    // Convert itemID_Key to a string for use in the OPath filter
    string hexItemID_Key = BitConverter.ToString (itemID_Key.Value);
    hexItemID_Key = "'0x" + hexItemID_Key.Replace ("-", String.Empty) + "'";

    // Build an opath filter expression.
    string query = "ItemID_Key=" + hexItemID_Key;

    return Item.FindOne (ctx, query);
}
```

Common Features

WinFS API provides several features across the entire spectrum of data classes. These features are

- Asynchrony

- Transactions

- Notifications

- Blob/stream support

- Cursoring and paging

Asynchrony

The WinFS API allows you to run queries asynchronously. The WinFS API uses the .NET standard asynchronous programming model patterns.

Transactions

The WinFS store is a transactional store. WinFS, therefore, allows you to make transactional updates to the store using the *BeginTransaction*, *CommitTransaction*, and *AbortTransaction* methods on the *ItemContext* object, as shown in the following example:

```
using (ItemContext ctx = ItemContext.Open()) {
  using (Transaction t = ctx.BeingTransaction()) {
    Person p = Person.FindOne (ctx,
        "PersonalNames[GivenName='Chandler' And SurName='Bing']" );
    Household h = Household.FindOne (ctx,
        "DisplayName = 'Chandler and Joey Household'");
    p.PersonalEAddresses.Add (new TelephoneNumber ("202", "555-1234"));
    p.Save ();
    h.Members.Add (p);
    h.Save ();
    t.Commit ();
  }
}
```

Notifications

The WinFS Notification Service uses the concepts of short-term and long-term subscriptions. A *short-term subscription* lasts until an application cancels the subscription or the application exits. A *long-term subscription* survives application restarts. WinFS API *watchers* are a set of classes that allow applications to be selectively notified of changes in the WinFS store and provide state information that can be persisted by the application to support suspend/resume scenarios.

The *Watcher* class can notify your application of changes to different aspects of WinFS objects, including the following:

- Item changes
- Embedded item changes
- Item extension changes
- Relationship changes

When a watcher raises an event, it sends watcher state data with the event notification. Your application can store this state data for later retrieval. Subsequently, you can use this watcher state data to indicate to WinFS that you want to receive events for all changes that occurred after the state was generated.

The watcher programming model also allows any combination of added, modified, and removed events to be disabled. It can also be configured to raise an initial event that simulates the addition of all existing items, item extensions, relationships, and so on.

The WinFS watcher design is broken down into the classes described in the following table.

Class	Purpose/Description
WatcherOptions	Class for specifying initial scope and granularity options to *StoreWatcher*
StoreWatcher	The quintessential class for watching WinFS items, embedded items, item extensions, and relationships
WatcherState	Opaque object that can be used to initialize a *StoreWatcher*
ChangedEventHandler	Class that defines the event handler to be called by *StoreWatcher*
ChangedEventArgs	Class passed as argument to *ChangedEventHandler*
ItemChangeDetail	Base class that provides granular change details for item events
ItemExtensionChangeDetail	Class derived from *ItemChangeDetail* that provides additional change details specific to item extension events
RelationshipChangeDetail	Class derived from *ItemChangeDetail* that provides additional change details specific to relationship events

You use the *StoreWatcher* class to create a watcher for some item in the WinFS store. The *StoreWatcher* instance will raise events when the specified item changes. You can specify the type of item and hierarchy to watch. By default, a watcher

- Does not raise an initial event to establish the current state

- Watches the item and the hierarchy (including immediate children) for any changes

- Raises add, remove, and modify events on this item or any child in entire hierarchy

- Raises add, remove, and modify events for item extensions on this item or any child in entire hierarchy

- Raises add, remove, and modify events for relationships in which this item or any child in entire hierarchy is the source of the relationship

Because by default a watcher watches for changes in the specified item and its descendants, you might want to specify *WatchItemOnly* as the watcher option. The following example watches for changes only to the located Person item:

```
Person p = Person.FindOne (ctx,
          "PersonalNames[GivenName='Rachel' and Surname='Emerald'");
StoreWatcher w = new StoreWatcher ( p, WatcherOptions.WatchItemOnly );
```

A Folder is just another WinFS item. You watch for changes in a Folder the same way you do for a Person:

```
Folder f = · · ·
StoreWatcher w = new StoreWatcher (f, <WatcherOptions>);
```

You can watch for changes in a specified relationship of an item, too:

```
Person p = · · ·
StoreWatcher w = new StoreWatcher (p, typeof(HouseholdMember),
                                   <WatcherOptions> );
w.ItemChanged += new ChangedEventHandler (ItemChangedHandler);
w.Enabled = true;

// Change notifications now arrive until we unsubscribe from the event
  ⋮
// Now we unsubscribe from the event
w.ItemChanged -= new ChangedEventHandler (ItemChangedHandler);
w.Dispose ();
  ⋮

// The change notification handler
void ItemChangedHandler (object source, ChangedEventArgs args) {
  foreach (ItemChangeDetail detail in args.Details) {
    switch (typeof(detail)) {
```

```
        case ItemExtensionChangeDetail:
          // handle added + modified + removed events for Item Extension
          break;

        case RelationshipChangeDetail:
          // handle added + modified + removed events for Relationship
          break;

        default:
        case ItemChangeDetail:
          // handle added + modified + removed events for Item or Embedded Item
          HandleItemChangeDetail (detail);
          break;
      }
    }
  |


void HandleItemChangeDetail (ItemChangeDetail detail) {
  switch (detail.ChangeType) {
    case Added:          // handle added event
      break;

    case Modified:       // handle modified event
      break;

    case Removed:        // handle modified event
            break;
  }
}
```

Blob and Stream Support

Blob and stream support APIs are still in flux at the time of this writing. Check the documentation for the latest information about how to access blobs and streams in the WinFS store.

Cursoring and Paging

The various *Find* methods in the WinFS classes can return a (potentially) large collection of objects. This collection is the equivalent of a rowset in the database world. Traditional database applications use a *paged cursor* to navigate efficiently within a large rowset. This cursor references a single row (a *thin cursor*) or a set of rows (a *page cursor*). The idea is that applications retrieve one page's worth of rows at a time; they can also pinpoint one row within the page for positioned update and delete. The WinFS API provides similar abstractions to the developer for dealing with large collections.

By default, a find operation provides a read-only, scrollable, dynamic cursor over the returned collection. An application can have a fire hose cursor for maximum performance. A fire hose cursor is a forward-only cursor. The application can retrieve a page of rows at a time, but the next retrieval operation will begin with the subsequent set of rows—it cannot go back and re-retrieve rows. In a sense, rows flow from the store to the application like water from a fire hose—hence the name.

The *CursorType* property in the *FindParameters* class will allow an application to choose between a fire hose and scrollable cursor. For both fire hose and scrollable cursors, the application can set a page size using the *PageSize* property of the *FindParameters* class. By default, the page size is set to 1.

Data Binding

You can use the WinFS data classes as data sources in a data-binding environment. The WinFS classes implement *IDataEntity* (for single objects) and *IDataCollection* (for collections) interfaces. The *IDataEntity* interface provides notifications to the data-binding target of changes to properties in the data source object. The *IDataCollection* interface allows the determination of the base type of an object in a polymorphic collection. It also allows you to retrieve a *System.Windows.Data.CollectionManager*, which navigates through the data entities of the collection and provides a view (for example, sort order or filter) of the collection. I discuss data binding in detail in Chapter 5.

Security

The WinFS security model fundamentally grants a set of *Rights* to a *Principal* on an *Item* in the following ways:

- Security is set at the level of *Items*.

- A set of rights can be granted to a security principle on an *Item*. This set includes: READ, WRITE, DELETE, EXECUTE (for all items), CREATE_CHILD, ADMINISTER, and AUDIT. (Additional rights are grantable on Folder items.)

- Users and applications are the security principles. Application rights supersede user rights. When an application doesn't have permission to delete a contact, a user cannot delete it via the application regardless of the user's permissions.

- Security is set using rules; each rule is a *Grant* and applies to a triplet: (*<ItemSet, PrincipalSet, RightSet>*).

- The rules are themselves stored as *Items*.

Getting Rights on an Item

Each WinFS item class has a method named *GetRightsForCurrentUser*, which returns the set of rights—READ, WRITE, DELETE, and so forth—that the current user has on the specified item. In addition, the method returns the set of methods that WinFS allows the user to execute.

Setting Rights on an Item

WinFS uses a special Item type, *SecurityRule*, to store permissions information on *Items*. Thus, setting and changing rights is no different from manipulating any other *Item* in WinFS. Here's a code example showing how to set rights on a folder item:

```
using (ItemContext ctx = ItemContext.Open("\\localhost\WinFS_C$")) {
  SecurityRule sr = new SecurityRule (ctx);
  sr.Grant = true;
  // set permission on items under folder1 including folder1
  sr.AppliesTo = <folder1's Identity Key>;
  sr.Condition = acl1;   // a DACL
  sr.Save();
}
```

Extending the WinFS API

Every built-in WinFS class contains standard methods such as *Find** and has properties for getting and setting field values. These classes and associated methods form the foundation of WinFS APIs and allow you to learn how to use one class and know, in general, how to use many other WinFS classes. However, while standard behavior is useful, each specific data type needs additional, type-specific behaviors.

Domain Behaviors

In addition to these standard methods, every WinFS type will typically have a set of domain-specific methods unique to that type. (Actually, WinFS documentation often refers to type definitions as *schema*, reflecting the database heritage of WinFS.) WinFS refers to these type-specific methods as *domain behaviors*. For example, here are some domain behaviors in the contacts schema:

- Determining whether an e-mail address is valid

- Given a folder, getting the collection of all members of the folder

- Given an item ID, getting an object representing this item

- Given a person, getting his or her online status

- Creating a new contact or a temporary contact with helper functions

Value-Added Behaviors

Data classes with domain behaviors form a foundation that application developers build on. However, it is neither possible nor desirable for data classes to expose every conceivable behavior related to that data.

You can provide new classes that extend the base functionality offered by the WinFS data classes. You do this by writing a class whose methods take one or more of the WinFS data classes as parameters. In the following example, the *OutlookMainServices* and *WindowsMessageServices* are hypothetical classes that use the standard WinFS *MailMessage* and *Person* classes:

```
MailMessage m = MailMessage.FindOne (…);
OutlookEMailServices.SendMessage(m);

Person p = Person.FindOne (…);
WindowsMessagerServices wms = new WindowsMessagerServices(p);
wms.MessageReceived += new MessageReceivedHandler (OnMessageReceived);
wms.SendMessage("Hello");
```

You can then register these custom classes with WinFS. The registration data will be associated with the schema metadata WinFS maintains for every installed WinFS type. WinFS stores your schema metadata as WinFS items; therefore, you can update, query, and retrieve it as you would all other WinFS items.

Specifying Constraints

The WinFS data model allows value constraints on types. WinFS evaluates and enforces these constraints when you add items to the store. However, you sometimes want to verify that input data satisfies its constraints without incurring the overhead of a roundtrip to the server. WinFS allows the schema/type author to decide whether the type supports client-side constraint checking. When a type supports client-side validation, the type will have a validate method you can call to verify that an object satisfies the specified constraints. Note that regardless of whether the developer calls the *Validate* method, WinFS still checks the constraints at the store.

Using the WinFS API and SQL

The WinFS API enables a developer to access the WinFS store by using familiar common language runtime (CLR) concepts. Throughout this chapter, I used the following coding pattern for WinFS access:

1. Bind to an *ItemContext*.

2. Find the desired items.

3. Update the items.

4. Save all changes back to the store.

Step 2 is essentially a query to the store. The WinFS API uses a filter expression syntax based on *OPath* for specifying these queries. In many cases, using filter expressions should be sufficient for most tasks. However, there will be cases where the developer will want to use the full power and flexibility of SQL.

The following capabilities are present in SQL, but they are not available when using a filter expression:

- Aggregation (*Group By, Having, Rollup*)

- Projection (including calculated select expressions, distinct, *Identity-Col, RowGuidCol*)

- For XML

- Union

- Option

- Right/full/cross join

- Nested selects

- Join to non-WinFS table

It is thus essential that a WinFS developer be able to seamlessly transition between the SQLClient API and the WinFS API, using one or the other in various places in the code.

Aggregate and Group with SQL, and Then Use WinFS API

A small-business owner, Joe, wants to determine who his top 10 customers are and send gift baskets to them. Assume that Customer is a schematized item type. This means that an ISV has provided a schema for the Customer type to WinFS, and therefore, it also means that a WinFS store can now contain Customer items. A Customer item has a holding link to a schematized Order Item type. Order Item has an embedded collection of Line Orders, as follows:

```
1. using (ItemContext ctx = ItemContext.Open()) {
2.
3.   SqlCommand cmd = ctx.CreateSqlCommand();
4.   cmd.CommandText =
5.   "select object(c) from Customers c inner join (" +
6.     "select top 10 C.ItemId, sum(p.price) " +
7.     "from Customers C" +
8.     "inner join Links L on L.SourceId = C.ItemId" +
9.   "inner join Orders O on L.TargetId = O.ItemId" +
10.    "cross join unnest(O.LineOrders) " +
11.    "group by C.ItemId" +
12.    "order by sum(p.price)) t ON c.ItemId = t.ItemId";
13.
14.   SqlDataReader rdr = cmd.ExecuteReader();
15.
16.   GiftBasketOrder gbOrder = new GiftBasketOrder(Ö);
17.
18.   while (rdr.Read()) {
19.     Customer c = new Customer((CustomerData) rdr.GetValue(0));
20.     // add the customer to gbOrder's recipient collection
21.     gbOrder.Recipients.Add(c);
22.   }
23.
24.   // send the order. The ISV's GiftBasketOrder can easily pull out
25.   // customer info such as shipping address from the Customer object
26.   gbOrder.Send();
27. }
```

In line 1 of this example, I open a context for the root of the system volume. In line 3, I create a SQL command object that I subsequently use to execute a SQL query against the WinFS store. This command object reuses the connection used by the item context. Lines 4 through 12 construct the query, and line 14 executes the query. The query returns the top 10 customers in the following manner: the SELECT statement in lines 6 through 12 generates a grouped table containing the total value of each customer's orders; the ORDER BY clause on line 12, combined with the TOP 10 modifier in line 6, selects only the top 10 customers in this grouped table.

The *GiftBasketOrder* class is a custom class that makes use of the WinFS API *Customer* object. I create an instance of *GiftBasketOrder* on line 16.

Line 19 uses the *SQLDataReader* to read the first column of the returned rowset and casts it to a *CustomerData* object.

When you define a new type in WinFS (known as creating a new schema), you are actually defining two types: your managed class and the WinFS store's persistent format of the class. WinFS always adds the *Data* suffix to the name of your class to create the name of the store's type. Therefore, for example, when you define a new Customer type that resides in the WinFS store, WinFS creates the parallel *CustomerData* WinFS User Defined Type (UDT).

The first column of the rowset contains the store's *CustomerData* object. I pass this object to the constructor of the *Customer* class, and the constructor initializes the new object from the *CustomerData* object. This example is typical of using store UDTs to construct WinFS API objects.

Line 24 adds the customer to the *Recipients* collection of the *GiftBasket-Order*.

Finally, I use the *Send* method on gbOrder to "send" this order.

Navigate in API, and Then Aggregate in SQL

Assume that you want to find the average salary (over a 10-year period) for the CEO of each company in my portfolio. Use the following assumptions:

- I have a folder named Companies In My Portfolio, which contains items of type Organization.

- *EmployeeData* is a link-based relationship, and it has a *Yearly-EmploymentHistory* that has the year and the salary for that year.

```
1.  using (ItemContext ctx = ItemContext.Open(@"Companies In My Portfolio")) {
2.
3.    SqlCommand cmd = ctx.CreateCommand();
4.    cmd.CommandText =
5.    "select avg( Salary ) from Links l cross apply " +
6.    "( select Salary from unnest( convert(" +
7.    "EmployeeData,l.LinkCol)::YearlyEmploymentHistory )" +
8.    "where Year >= '1993' ) where l.LinkID = @LinkID";
9.
10.   SqlParameter param = new SqlParameter ("@LinkID", SqlDbType.BigInt);
11.   cmd.Parameters.Add (param);
12.
13.   Folder f = Folder.FindByPath (ctx, ".");
14.
15.   FindResult orgs = f.GetMembersOfType (typeof(Organization));
16.   foreach (Organization o in orgs) {
17.     EmployeeData ed = EmployeeData.FindEmployeeInRole (o,
18.             Organization.Categories.CeoRole);
19.     param.Value = ed.Link.LinkID;
20.     SqlDataReader rdr = cmd.ExecuteReader ();
21.     rdr.Read ();
22.     Console.WriteLine ("{0} ${1}",
23.       ((Person)ed.Target).PersonalNames[0].FullName, rdr.GetFloat(0) );
24.     rdr.Close ();
25.   }
26.  }
```

Line 1 opens a context for the Companies In My Portfolio WinFS share. Lines 3 through 11 create a parameterized SQL query that I can use in the context of the folder. This query returns the average salary for a given employee (represented by the *@LinkID* parameter). Lines 10 and 11 specify that *@LinkID* is a parameter of type *BigInt*. I execute this query later in the example, on line 20.

Line 13 gets a *Folder* object that represents the folder indicated by the share that I specified when creating the context. Lines 15 and 16 set up the loop for going through the collection of *Organization* objects in this folder.

For each organization, line 17 gets the *EmployeeData* object for the CEO.

Line 19 prepares for the query and sets the value of the parameter to the appropriate LinkID, and then line 20 executes the parameterized SELECT.

Line 21 reads the next and only row from the query result, and lines 22 and 23 print the name of the CEO and the 10-year average salary.

Summary

The WinFS data store provides a far richer data storage model than traditional file systems. Because it supports data, behavior, and relations, it's difficult to categorize WinFS as a file system, a relational database, or an object database. It's a bit of all those technologies in one product. WinFS provides a common definition of ubiquitous information that is globally visible and available to all applications running on Longhorn. Applications can leverage the query, retrieval, transactional update, and filtering capabilities of WinFS; therefore, the developer spends less time developing data access and storage code and more time working on unique application functionality.

5

Data Binding

Data binding in its traditional sense means associating some underlying data with one or more user interface elements. The data provides the information to display. The user interface elements render the information in the appropriate format.

Longhorn extends the traditional idea of data binding in a number of ways. You can bind a property of a user interface element to a property of any common language runtime (CLR) object, or to an attribute of an XML node.

The data binding can be unidirectional (in either direction) or bidirectional. For example, traditional data binding has the information in the data source flow to its bound user interface element. Alternatively, the information in the user interface element can flow back to the data source. Bidirectional data binding, of course, supports information flow in each direction and enables user input via user interface element to update the data in the data source.

Data binding can also be static (one time only) or dynamic. With static data binding, the information transfer occurs when you initially create the data binding. Subsequent changes to values in the data do not affect the value in the user interface element. Dynamic data binding allows changes to data in the data source to propagate to the User Interface element and vice versa.

Longhorn data binding also supports transformation of the data as it flows to and from the data source and user interface elements. This transformation enables the application author to add UI semantics to the data.

Some typical transformations might be the following:

- Displaying negative numbers in red and positive numbers in black
- Displaying images based on a contact being online or offline

- Creating dynamic bar charts by binding a rectangle's height to a stock price

- Animating the position of an image by binding its coordinates to a property of a CLR object

Longhorn data binding is also fundamentally asynchronous. A user interface element receives an event when a new data source binds to the element. In addition, as a data source collects its data, it fires events to indicate that its contents have changed.

One can data-bind to any CLR object or XMLnode, and hence one can easily data-bind to various data models in Longhorn—CLR objects, XML, ADO.NET Datasets, Web service messages, or WinFS objects. Longhorn also provides a number of built-in data source classes that allow you to easily and declaratively bring data asynchronously into an application. There are specific data sources for XML, .NET objects, ADO.NET datasets, and WinFS objects. The data source model is extensible, so you can create your own custom data source classes when necessary.

Creating a Data Binding

You can bind a dynamic property of a user interface element to a property of any CLR object. To do this, you must describe the desired correspondence between some item of a data source and the target user-interface element. Each such correspondence, or binding, must specify the following:

- The data source item

- The path to the appropriate value in the data source item

- The target user-interface element

- The appropriate property of the target user-interface element

The Data Binding

The Framework represents a data binding by an instance of the *MSAvalon.Data.Bind* class. This class has a number of properties that control the data binding: *Path*, *BindType*, *UpdateType*, *Transformer*, *Culture*, *BindFlags*, and *Source*.

You set the *Path* property to a string that specifies the property or value in the data source to which the bind object binds. The *BindType* property controls the direction and frequency of the data bind. It must be one of three values:

OneWay, *TwoWay*, and *OneTime*. A *OneWay* bind type causes the data binding to transfer new values from the data source to the target property but it does not propagate changes in the target property back to the data source. A *TwoWay* bind type propagates changes in both directions. When you specify the *OneTime* bind type, the data binding transfers the value from the data source to the target property only when you first activate the binding.

You can set the *Transformer* property to any object that implements the *IDataTransformer* interface. When the data binding propagates a value, it passes the value through the transformer. The transformer examines the incoming value and produces a new value as output. Note that the input and output values don't need to be the same type. You could have an integer flag as input and produce different image files as output.

The *UpdateType* property determines when changes to the target property propagate back to the data source when the bind type is *TwoWay*. You can specify one of three values: *Immediate* means propagate the new value to the data source immediately after the target property changes; *OnLostFocus* means propagate the value when the target control loses the input focus; and *Explicit* says to wait until code calls the bind object and tells it to propagate the new value.

The *Source* property references the source data item of the binding. You can use the *DataSource*, *ElementSource*, *DataContextSource*, or *ObjectSource* attributes to set the bind object's *Source* property. You use the *ElementSource* attribute to set the *Source* to an Element by providing the element ID as the value of the *ElementSource* attribute. The *DataContextSource* attribute allows you to set the *Source* to the data context of another element by setting the element ID to the *DataContextSource*. You use the *ObjectSource* attribute to specify an object as the source of the binding. Finally, the *DataSource* attribute allows you to set the *Source* to the *Data* property of the *DataSource*. This will be discussed in detail in "The Data Source Item" section.

The *Culture* property allows you to specify a *CultureInfo* for bindings that need to be culture-aware.

The *BindFlags* property supports a single nonzero value: *NotifyOnTransfer*. It's very important to understand that a data binding is inherently asynchronous. When you change the value in the data source, the corresponding target property doesn't receive the updated value right away. It might take an arbitrary amount of time before the new value propagates to the target property. When you need to know when the binding has completed updating the target property, you set the *BindFlags* property to the *NotifyOnTransfer* value. The data binding will then fire the *MSAvalon.Data.DataTransfer* event after updating the target property.

Defining a Binding Expression Using Code

You can create a data binding programmatically, although I expect you'll rarely need or want to do so. Simply create an instance of the *Bind* class and call the method *SetBinding*. Here's one possible example:

```
using MSAvalon.Data;

Bind binding = new Bind ();
binding.Path = path;
binding.BindType = bindType;
binding.Source = source;
binding.UpdateType = updateType;

element.SetBinding (property, binding);
```

Alternatively, here's another way to write the prior code using one of the Bind class's convenience constructors:

```
using MSAvalon.Data;

Bind binding = new Bind (path, bindType, source, updateType);
element.SetBinding (property, binding);
```

You could use other convenience methods, such as the *SetBinding* method on an element, and simplify the prior code to this:

```
element.SetBinding (property, path, bindType, source, updateType);
```

Defining a Binding Expression Using Markup

I expect you'll prefer to define most data bindings using markup. All the previous concepts still apply—you create a *Bind* object, set its properties to the appropriate values, and associate it with a property of a target element. For example, the following markup creates a *Bind* object as the value of the Button object's *Text* property.

```
<DockPanel xmlns="http://schemas.microsoft.com/2003/xaml" />
  <DockPanel.Resources>
    <myNameSpace:Person def:Name="MyPerson" Name="Bob"/>
  </DockPanel.Resources> . . .
  <Button>
    <Button.Content>
      <Bind Path="Name" BindType="OneWay" ObjectSource="{MyPerson}" />
    </Button.Content>
  </Button>
```

To associate a data binding with a particular user interface element's property, you use the data binding as the value of the property. In the example just shown, the data binding binds the resource called *MyPerson* to the *Text* property of the *Button* element because I defined the data binding between the *Button.Text* start and end tags.

The *DockPanel Resources* property declares that the following child elements are resources. Unlike regular XAML elements, which are instantiated when the runtime parses the XAML file, the runtime does not instantiate a resource until you actually use it.

In the prior example, the *Source* of the bindings is a *Person* object, therefore the *Bind* instance references this *Person* object instance.

The *Path* attribute specifies the path within the data source item to the value of interest. In the prior example, the path is simply *Name*, so the binding retrieves the *Name* property of the *Person* instance. However, the path could be more complex. For example, if the *Name* property returned an object with additional structure, the path could be something like *Name.FirstName*.

The prior example showed how to define a data binding using a complex property definition for the *Button.Text* property's value. However, you can use an alternative, and considerably more compact, definition for a data-binding expression. In this case, you define a string as the data-binding expression. The string begins with an asterisk character, which the XAML compiler interprets as an escape character, and then the name of the class to instantiate, and then, enclosed in parentheses, a series of semicolon-separated name value pairs.

```
<DockPanel >
  ⋮
 <Button Text="*Bind(Path=Name;BindType=OneWay)" />
  ⋮
</DockPanel>
```

When you define a data binding but don't specify a value for the *Source* property (using *DataSource, ElementSource, DataContextSource or Object-Source*), the data binding retrieves the data source from the *DataContext* property for the current element. When the current element has no *DataContext*, the binding object retrieves the parent element's *DataContext* recursively. This allows you to define a data source once on the appropriate element in your markup and then use that data source in various bindings on child elements.

In the following example, I set the *DataContext* property of the *Dock-Panel* element to a data binding that references my data source. Effectively, all child elements inherit this *DataContext* property when they don't otherwise set it to a different value. Because the data bindings on the *Button* elements do not specify a value for the *Source* property, the binding uses the source from the inherited *DataContext*. Of course, you can always specify a source to cause a particular data binding to use a different data source.

```
<DockPanel xmlns="http:////schemas.microsoft.com//2003//xaml//"
           DataContext="{MyPerson}">
  ⋮
   <Button Text='*Bind(Path="Name";BindType="OneWay")' />
   <Button Text='*Bind(Path="Age";BindType="OneWay")' />
  ⋮
</DockPanel>
```

Data Binding Types

A particular data binding can be of three types: *OneTime*, *OneWay*, and *Two-Way*. You set the *BindType* property to one of those enumerated values when you declare the binding.

One-Time Data Binding

When you request one-time data binding, the runtime, using the data source and the specified path, retrieves the source value and initializes the specified target property to that value. Normally, nothing happens subsequently when the source or the target property change value.

However, there are two special cases. When the *DataContext* of an element changes, effectively, the data source has changed and therefore the binding performs another one-time transfer. In addition, in many cases, the data context refers to a collection of objects. When the current object for a collection changes, the data binding performs a one-time transfer.

One-Way Data Binding

When you request one-way data binding, the runtime retrieves the source value and initializes the specified target property to that value. Each time the source value changes the data binding retrieves the new value and reinitializes the target property.

Two-Way Data Binding

When you request two-way data binding, the runtime retrieves the source value and initializes the specified target property to that value. Each time the source value changes, the data binding retrieves the new value and reinitializes the target property. In addition, when the target property changes value—for example, when the user types into an edit control—the data binding retrieves the new target property value and propagates it back to the source. Two-way data binding is the default type of a data binding.

Transformers

A transformer allows you to convert a value from one form to another as it propagates to and from a data source to a target. You might use a transformer to convert a value from its internal representation to a unique displayed value. For example, you can use a transformer to display a negative floating-point number using red text and a positive number using black text. You can also display different icons for various credit-worthy ratings for a customer.

You can also use a transformer as a data type converter. For example, your source value could be a *Point* object, while the property to which you want to bind the value requires a *Length* instance.

A transformer also receives the culture information for the user interface as one of its parameters. You can use this information to tailor the presented user interface to the current culture of the user—for example, you can provide different icons when running under different cultures.

The *IDataTransformer* Interface

A transformer is any object that implements the *IDataTransformer* interface. Here's the definition of the interface:

```
interface IDataTransformer {
  object Transform (object o, DependencyID id, CultureInfo culture);
  object InverseTransform (object o, PropertyInfo pInfo, CultureInfo culture);
}
```

A data binding calls the *Transform* method when propagating a source value to a target property. Parameter *o* is the source value, parameter *id* identifies the target property, and parameter *culture* identifies the culture for the transformation.

The data binding calls the *InverseTransform* method when propagating a changed target property value back to the source. In this case, parameter *o* is the changed target property's value and *pInfo* identifies the type to which to convert the value. As before, *culture* is the culture for the transformation.

Both methods allow you to return *null* to indicate that the binding should not propagate a value in the respective direction. Here is a simple transformer that returns a color based on an integer value:

```
<SimpleText Text="*Bind(Path=Name)"
Foreground="*Bind(Path=Age; Transformer=AgeToColorTransformer)"/>

public class AgeToColorTransformer: IDataTransformer {
  public object Transform (object o, DependencyID di, CultureInfo culture) {
    int age = (int) o;
    if (age < 0 || age > 120) return Grey;
```

```
      if (age <= 30) return Green;
      if (age <= 70) return Gold;
      if (age <= 120) return Red;
  }
  public object InverseTransform (object o, PropertyInfo i, CultureInfo c) {
      return null;
  }
}
```

Providing Property Change Notifications

The CLR does not provide a generic way for an object to notify its clients that one of its properties has changed. Nevertheless, a dynamic binding requires such notifications so that the binding can propagate changed property values to the target dynamic property. Longhorn introduces the *IPropertyChange* interface to allow an object to signal when one of its properties changes value. Note that the interface defines a single event of type *PropertyChangedEventHandler* and that the event handler can retrieve the name of the changed property using the *PropertyName* property of the second parameter to the handler.

```
interface IPropertyChange {
  event PropertyChangedEventHandler PropertyChanged;
}

delegate void PropertyChangedEventHandler (object sender,
                                           PropertyChangedEventArgs e);

class PropertyChangedEventArgs : EventArgs {
  public virtual string PropertyName { get ;}
}
```

In the following code, I've rewritten the *Person* class from earlier in the chapter to support changing the *Name* and *Age* properties and to fire the appropriate events when such changes occur.

```
namespace MyNamespace {
  public class Person : IPropertyChange {
    private string m_name;
    private int    m_age;
    public event PropertyChangedEventHandler PropertyChanged;

    public string Name {
      get { return m_name; }
      set {
        if (m_name != value) {
          m_name = value;
```

```
          RaisePropertyChangeEvent ("Name");
        }
      }
    }
    public int Age {
      get { return m_age; }
      set {
        if (m_age != value) {
          m_age = value;
          RaisePropertyChangeEvent ("Age");
        }
      }
    }

    private void RaisePropertyChangedEvent (string propertyName) {
      if (PropertyChanged != null)
        PropertyChanged (this, new PropertyChangedEventArgs (propertyName));
    }

    public Person (string name, int age) {
      m_name = name; m_age = age;
    }
  }
}
```

Your object implements this interface by calling the *PropertyChanged* delegate whenever one of its "interesting" properties changes value. Note that you need to invoke the delegate only when a property used in a dynamic binding changes value. Your object can have properties for which you do not fire change notifications.

For performance reasons, you should fire the change notifications only when the property has really changed value. When the object doesn't know which property changed value, it can request that all bindings to any property on itself be updated, or it can pass *String.Empty* for the changed property name.

The Data Source Item

Longhorn provides a set of built-in data sources, which enables you to easily and declaratively get data into the application asynchronously and without blocking UI.

A data source item is any object that implements the *IDataSource* interface.

```
interface IDataSource {
    public virtual Object Data { get; }
    public virtual void Refresh()
}
```

This interface has a *Data* property that lets the binding get the data from the data source item. The *Refresh* method allows the binding to request that the data source item retrieve its data when it's not available. Longhorn provides a number of data source classes, and you'll see some of them shortly.

Generally, a data source implementation also provides a strongly typed property that returns the native API of the data provider. For example, the *Sql-DataSource* and *XmlDataSource* classes provide the *DataSet* and *Document* properties, respectively:

```
class SqlDataSource : IDataSource, … {
    ⋮
    DataSet         DataSet { get; }
    ⋮
}
class XmlDataSource : IDataSource, … {
    ⋮
    XmlDocument     Document { get; }
    ⋮
}
```

Therefore, if you really have to, you can directly access the underlying data provider.

Using Any CLR Object as a Data Source

The *ObjectDataSource* class allows you to create an instance of a specified type as a data source item. Commonly, you'll use XAML and declare your data sources as resources in your markup. For example, assume that I have the following definition of a *Person* class in an assembly called *MyAssembly* and that I'd like to use an instance of this class as a data source item:

```
namespace MyNamespace {
  public class Person {
    private string m_name;
    private int m_age;

    public string Name { get { return m_name; } }
    public int Age { get { return m_age; } }

    public Person (string name, int age) {
      m_name = name; m_age = age;
    }
  }
}
```

The *Person* class doesn't need any additional support to be a data source item. I can use an instance of the *ObjectDataSource* class as the data source item and inform it that the underlying data provider should be an instance of the *Person* class. To do this, I can use markup to declare an instance of an *ObjectData-Source* as a XAML resource.

```
<DockPanel>
  <DockPanel.Resources>
    <ObjectDataSource def:Name ="source1"
        TypeName="MyNamespace.Person, MyAssembly, Version=1.0.0.0, Culture=neutr
al, PublicKeyToken=0123456789abcdef"
        Parameters="Brent, 0x30" />
  </DockPanel.Resources>
</DockPanel>
```

As always, XAML element names represent Framework class names. Therefore, the *ObjectDataSource* element says to create an instance of the *ObjectDataSource* class. The value of the *def:Name* attribute is the name of this resource ("*source1*" in the preceding example).

The *ObjectDataSource* instance will create a new instance of the class referred to by *TypeName* either by calling its default constructor or, when you specify the *Parameters* attribute, by calling the constructor that best matches the signature of the value of the *Parameter* attribute.

Recall that markup is equivalent to code, so the preceding markup is the same as the following code:

```
ObjectDataSource source1 = new ObjectDataSource();
source1.TypeName = "MyNamespace.Person, MyAssembly, Version=1.0.0.0,
                    Culture=neutral, PublicKeyToken=0123456789abcdef";
source1.Parameters = "Brent, 0x30";
```

The *ObjectDataSource* class also provides mechanisms to call methods on objects and refer to existing objects in addition to simply instantiating a new object.

Using a Data Source with Data Binding

One can declare a data source as a resource in the *Resources* property of an element or the application level resources. Any data source declared in the Application resources can be used across the application in any page. A data source defined in the resources of an element can be used only within the scope of the element.

```
<DockPanel
  <DockPanel.Resources>
    <ObjectDataSource def:Name="source1"
        TypeName="MyNamespace.Person, MyAssembly, …"
        Parameters="Brent, 0x30" />
  </DockPanel.Resources>
```

```
     ⋮
  <Button Text="*Bind(Path=Name ; BindType= OneWay; DataSource = {source1}"/>
  <Button DataContext="*Bind(DataSource={source1})" Text="*Bind(Path=Name)"/>
     ⋮
</DockPanel>
```

In the example just shown, the data binding binds the data source called *source1*. You can set the *DataSource* attribute to the resource ID of a XAML Resource. When the resource implements the *IDataSource* interface, the runtime will set the *Source* property of the *Bind* instance to the object returned by the *Data* property of the specified *DataSource* resource. When the resource does not implement the *IDataSource* interface, the runtime sets the *Source* property of the binding to the resource object itself.

In the prior example, the *DataSource* attribute references an *ObjectData-Source* resource. Therefore, the binding requests the *Data* property from the *ObjectDataSource*. The data source, in turn, instantiates the *Person* class as specified in the markup.

In the first Button, the *Source* property of the *Bind* instance references this *Person* object instance. The path is simply *Name*, so the binding retrieves the *Name* property of the *Person* instance.

In the second Button, *DataContext* is bound to the *ObjectDataSource*. This action will set *DataContext* of the Button to the *Person* object so that any bindings on Button will use the *Person* object as the default source for their bindings.

One can similarly data-bind to any of the available data sources. Some of the other data sources shipped with Longhorn are mentioned in paragraphs that follow. Others, such as data sources to get data from Web services, will be coming online.

Using XML as a Data Source

The *XmlDataSource* class is a data source that uses an XML Document Object Model (DOM) as the underlying data provider. You can use markup to create the DOM from a Uniform Resource Locator (URL) referencing an XML stream. You can also create the DOM by supplying the XML inline with the markup as the following example demonstrates:

Using URI

```
<DockPanel>
  <DockPanel.Resources>
    <XmlDataSource def:Name="source2"
        Source="http://www.wiseowl.com/People.xml"
        XPath="/People/Person[@Age>21]" />
```

Using inline markup

```
<XmlDataSource def:Nsme="source3"
  XPath="/People/Person[@Age>50]" >
  <People>
      <Person Name='Bambi' Age='61'>
      <Person Name='Bozo' Age='54'>
      <Person Name='Brent' Age='48'>
      ⋮
  </People>
</XmlDataSource>
</DockPanel.Resources>
</DockPanel>
```

Using a *DataSet* as a Data Source

The *SqlDataSource* class is a data source that uses a *DataSet* as the underlying data provider. It creates a *DataSet* and fills it by executing a SQL command on the database.

```
<DockPanel>
  <DockPanel.Resources>
    <SqlDataSource def:Name="source4">
      ConnectionString="server=localhost;Database=UserGroup"
      SelectCommand="SELECT * FROM Members" />
    </SqlDataSource>
  <DockPanel.Resources>
</DockPanel>
```

Alternatively, you can use the *ObjectDataSource* class and bind to a strongly typed *DataSet*-derived class that you've defined in a code-behind file.

```
<DockPanel>
  <DockPanel.Resources >
  <ObjectDataSource def:Name="sds1"
    Type="MyDataset"/>
  </ObjectDataSource>
 </DockPanel.Resources>
</DockPanel>
```

Using Windows Storage as a Data Source

The WinFS*DataSource* class uses WinFS as the underlying data provider. You can use it to bind to the everyday information maintained by Microsoft Windows Storage.

```
<DockPanel>
  <DockPanel.Resources>
    <WinFSDataSource ContextString="c:\">
      <WinFSDataSource.Query
```

```
        Type="Person" Filter="DisplayName='Ted'" Sort="DisplayName ASC">
            <Query.ProjectionOptions Field="DisplayName" />
            <Query.ProjectionOptions Field="Birthdate">
              <Projection.ProjectionOptions … />
            </Query.ProjectionOptions>
          </ WinFSDataSource.Query>
        </WinFSDataSource>
      </DockPanel.Resources>
    </DockPanel>
```

Using a Custom Data Source

You can also specify a custom class as a data source. The class must implement the *IDataSource* interface. You'll typically want to associate an XML namespace prefix with your custom class's namespace, and then use the prefix-qualified class name in the markup as usual:

```
<Canvas … >
  ⋮
  <Canvas.Resources>
    <WO:InfraredDataSource def:Name="source8"
        PropA='value1'
        PropB='value2'
    </WO:InfraredDataSource>
  </Canvas.Resources>
</Canvas>
```

Summary

Data binding provides an easy and efficient method to connect information to a user interface element that displays the data. You get automatic propagation of the values in either direction, one time or repeatedly, with the ability to convert the data representation on the fly when needed. And you can do so with little or no programmatic coding using markup. Data binding allows you to get the data where you want it and move on to writing the rest of your application.

6

Communication

In the past decade, connectivity between computers has become ubiquitous. Ten years ago most personal computers were not attached to a network. In fact, the idea of communicating to another computer typically meant that the user initiated a dial-up connection to a bulletin board system (BBS), and that user's personal computer pretended to be a dumb terminal, simply displaying information from the remote system. As Internet usage grew, users became used to connecting—again, typically via a dial-up connection—to the Internet. The computer pretended to be a not-quite-so-dumb terminal that served as a Web browser and displayed rich media content: text, graphics, animations, and eventually video.

As network and Internet connectivity became ubiquitous, developers started producing applications that expected and, in fact, required such connectivity. Some examples are application such as Microsoft Windows Messenger, numerous e-mail clients, newsgroup readers, peer-to-peer applications, and many more. It's not uncommon today for normal desktop applications that don't actually need a network connection to use a connection when present to notify the user when a new version of the application is available.

Unfortunately, developing an application that communicates with other applications has traditionally been rather difficult. The developer of a communicating application needs to deal with numerous difficulties: firewalls, address boundaries, routing issues, authentication and authorization, data security, differing protocols, differing data representations, and more. Longhorn's communication services generally handle all these difficulties for you, allowing you to focus on developing your custom application functionality.

Types of Communication Services

Let's look at various types of applications a platform should support.

Private Network Services

Many network-aware applications never attempt to communicate to systems outside of some internal network. For example, many corporate applications communicate solely with one or more internal servers on the corporate network. In this tightly controlled environment, a developer can typically assume a common network protocol, security domain, authentication and authorization scheme, and often, development platform. Interoperability with foreign platforms is not a requirement. The number of users is often relatively small—at least when compared to the number of users on the Internet as a whole.

Private Network to Private Network Services

When an application on one private network needs to communicate with an application on a different private network, complications arise. A business-to-business (B2B) application is a typical example of such an application. Company A's purchasing system would like to place an order with Company B's order entry system. In this situation, the purchasing application would typically run on one private network, the order entry application would run on a different private network, and the companies would use the Internet as the bridge between the two private networks.

This introduces a few complications in the connectivity. Because the communication occurs over the public Internet, data security becomes an issue. To establish secure communications between the applications, the two companies will typically need to implement authentication, authorization, and possibly, encryption services. These requirements aren't trivial, even when both companies use the same platform. However, the more common scenario is that the two companies do not use the same platforms and operating systems, meaning that the applications will very likely not have a common security infrastructure.

Of course, neither company has any control of the public portion of the network connection. The Internet is well known for its high latencies, but it's not quite as well known that certain types of messages can be dropped entirely. A robust application might need to handle these scenarios. In addition, limitations in transports and encodings might exist if there is a different platform on each side of a conversation.

Protocol Bridges

Over time, companies often want to connect existing applications to each other and to new applications. Existing systems often use disparate protocols, platforms, and data interchange formats. New applications must interoperate with existing deployed systems. This scenario has many similar requirements as the previous business-to-business scenario. In addition, interoperability to existing applications often requires support for protocols other than Transmission Control Protocol/Internet Protocol (TCP/IP), the standard protocol used on the Internet.

End User Communication Applications

The previously described, communication-based applications typically run within a corporate environment—from server to server, within a company, or across companies. However, end user systems also run communications applications. A traditional client-server application runs on the client and initiates communication with a server. A server can communicate back to its clients only after the client has connected to it. A server cannot arbitrarily establish a connection to a client. A new, but growing area of communications applications is a *client-to-client application*, also known as a peer-to-peer application. Many games, instant messengers, and file-sharing applications support direct communication from one client application to another client application. Collaboration applications also typically share data by using peer-to-peer communications. Some applications combine client-server and peer-to-peer applications. Instant messenger applications typically contact a central server to receive presence notifications about a person, but they connect directly to the person's instant messenger application to send a file to that person.

What Is Indigo?

Indigo is an implementation of a messaging system that enables secure, reliable, transacted messaging over multiple transports and across heterogeneous systems.

Two Forms of Communication

An application that uses the Indigo messaging services is called, not surprisingly, an Indigo service application. Indigo service applications support two main communications types: a *stateless model*, in which messages are received with few if any guarantees, and a *stateful model*, which creates a communication session between two service objects. The stateless model is equivalent to current-day Web services and is useful when broadcasting noncritical information. The stateful model, on the other hand, uses session state to enable Web services to provide functionality across the Internet, including callback methods, events, widely distributed transactions, and reliability and durability guarantees that enterprise applications require.

Reliability and Durability

Once a session has been established between two service instances, Indigo provides delivery assurances about messages within the session to insulate applications from transient communications problems. You can require that messages arrive at least once, at most once, or exactly once and that they arrive in the order in which they were sent. The default session configuration ensures that messages arrive exactly once and in the order in which they were sent.

Indigo can also persist service instance data and messages to support long-running services and to protect against the consequences of a service application failure. Services that indicate which instance data should be persisted can be stored after a period of inactivity and be reactivated with their state restored when another message arrives. In addition, messages are persisted on arrival and departure. Should an application failure occur, a durable service can resurrect itself and pick up processing messages where its predecessor left off.

Message-Based Activation

Indigo service applications can be hosted in any type of application, but services hosted in ASP.NET can be activated automatically when a message arrives for them. This not only enables automatic startup, but also means that long-running services that persist instance data can be stored on disk, to be reactivated with their state data restored when a message for them arrives after a long period. In addition, Indigo service applications can be activated using an extensible protocol layer that supports HTTP, TCP/IP, and cross-process protocols out of the box.

The Indigo Architecture

The Indigo framework is a layered architecture. You generally interact with the top layer (known as the *service layer*) and work in terms of program abstractions—methods, events, and callbacks. The service layer converts these abstractions into messages, which it delivers to lower layers—a process that eventually result in the message transmission.

The SOAP specification defines messages at the XML Infoset level. The XML Infoset defines a hierarchical structure for information. Specifically, it does not require that information be represented by angle-bracket-encapsulated data. Angle-bracket encapsulation just happens to be one particular serialization format for an XML Infoset. Soap requires a sender to pass an XML Infoset to a receiver; however, the actual serialization of the XML Infoset could be text or some other representation. It's the job of the formatter to convert an Infoset to and from a particular serialized representation.

SOAP does specify how a message gets from one place to another. Delivery and receipt of messages is the function of the transport layer, which deals with wire-level details. The transport layer defines abstract classes and interfaces you can use to implement any wire protocol. The transport layer also provides default implementations of those interfaces for TCP and Hypertext Transfer Protocol (HTTP) wire protocols.

Figure 6-1 shows the layered architecture of the Indigo system. The following sections describe each layer in more detail.

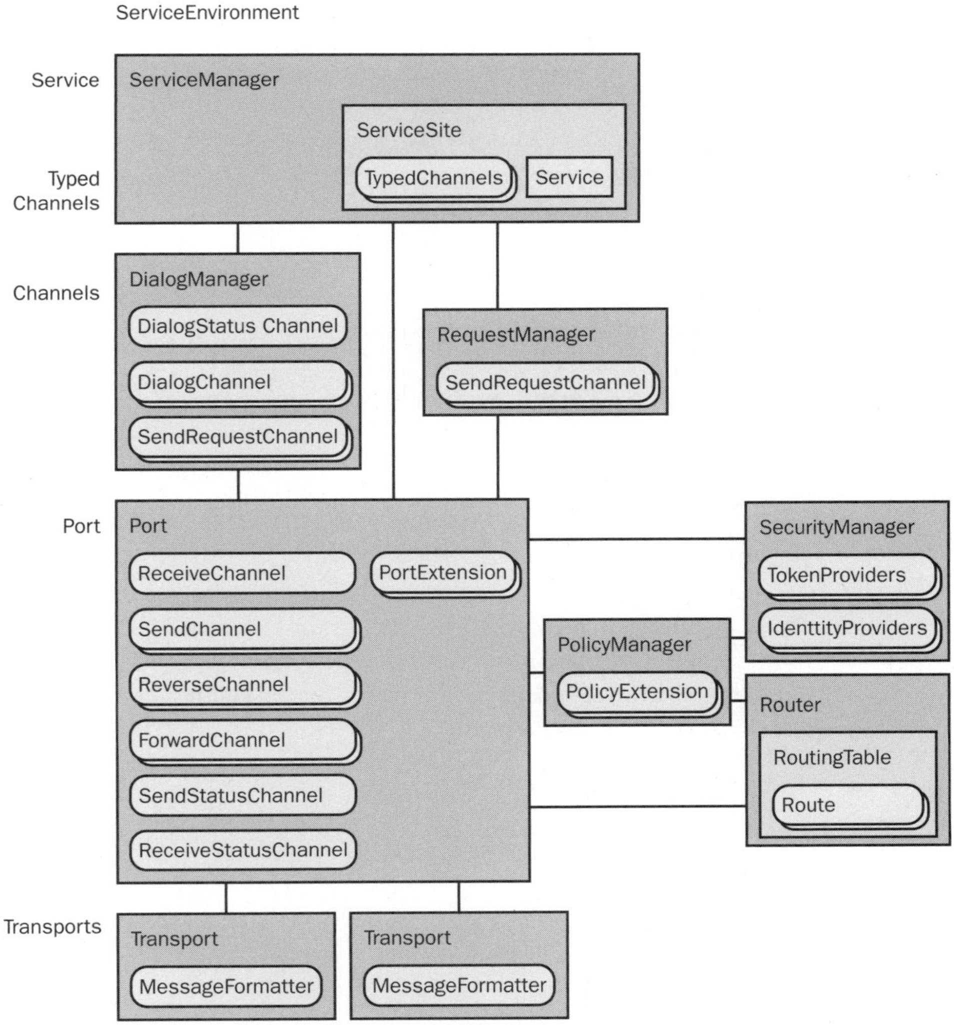

Figure 6-1   The Indigo architecture and important classes

The Service Layer

The service layer is the top-most layer in the Indigo architecture and provides a managed application programming interface (API) to both the service and client applications. It contains the classes that provide the basis for building services using the system-provided implementations. Using the service layer enables you to harness the power of the underlying layers without needing to understand the details of their implementation.

The service layer is a set of managed classes that implement strongly typed message sending and receiving. Your application calls a method with a return value when it wants to send a message and receive a response to that message (known as a *correlated message pair*). Similarly, your application implements an event handler, and the Indigo services call your event handler when a service receives the appropriate message. While you can process the actual messages directly, it's much easier to use traditional methods, events, and callbacks and let the underlying serialization system build, send, read, and convert messages.

Typed Channels

The methods provided by the service layer translate the method calls to and from a message-based protocol. The service layer passes strongly typed messages to a typed channel. A typed channel exchanges strongly typed messages by using a general messaging pattern, depending on the kind of typed channel. For example, a datagram typed channel sends a strongly typed message without any guarantees of delivery. A dialog exchange typed channel sends a strongly typed message with reliable delivery. There will typically be a typed-channel for each type of message you send or receive.

Untyped Channels

A typed channel sends its messages using an untyped channel. Basically, the typed channel provides the type-safe wrapper around use of the untyped channel. It's actually the untyped channel that implements a particular message exchange pattern—either datagram or dialog exchange. An untyped channel sends its messages via a port.

Ports

A port exchanges messages from untyped channels to the underlying transport and vice versa. A port contains a pipeline of one or more untyped channels that process messages from and to the transport and the untyped channel.

Transports and Formatters

A transport represents an adapter for an underlying wire protocol, such as TCP or HTTP. The transport handles connections, addressing, and flow control, but it delegates serializing of a message to a formatter. Conceptually, a transport accepts a message from a port, requests a formatter to serialize the message into a particular wire format, and sends the formatted message using a particular adapter. Of course, it also performs the inverse operations.

Transports receive messages from or pass messages to their associated Port message pipeline. Transports are the only objects in the hierarchy that deal with message formats. All higher levels always handle message objects. You can see this structure in Figure 6-1, which shows the layer architecture of the Indigo system.

Managers

The Indigo manager objects provide most, if not all, of the complex functionality supported by Indigo service applications. When an application makes what seems like a simple request to the service layer—for example, "Send this message, and wait for the response"—a complex series of messages might result. For example, the system might time out while waiting for the response and might need to resend the request. Or the request might require sending authentication messages to the recipient. Whatever the situation, the managers handle the complexities resulting from your application requests. Managers often inject port extensions into the port message pipeline and take ownership of messages they need to process to provide the service your application requests. Figure 6-2 provides a picture of how managers interact with the port and untyped channels.

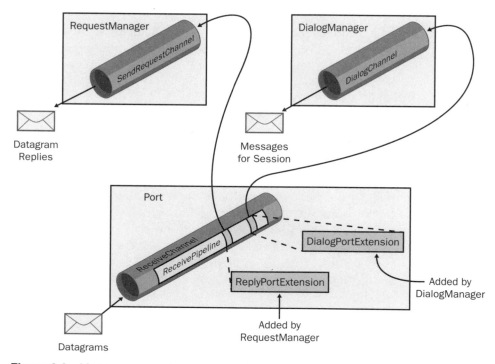

Figure 6-2   Managers acquiring messages from a port

Indigo Applications

The Indigo infrastructure enables you to create a wide variety of applications. You can create something as simple as a chat application that operates between two peers on an intranet and as complex as a scalable Web service for millions of users. And just as the complexities of such applications vary so widely, so do the features of Indigo. In other words, the Indigo infrastructure is also highly variable, and you need to use only those parts that are appropriate to the complexity of your solution.

Indigo service applications are one or both sides of a SOAP message exchange. The simplest example of an Indigo application resembles an XML Web service built with ASP.NET, an .asmx page. This type of application is known as a *Indigo Web service application*. You can also build Indigo applications that can create complex, two-way conversations between two objects in much the same way you can use proxies to remote classes in .NET remoting. This type of application is known as an *Indigo RemoteObject service application*.

Indigo Web Service Applications

Indigo Web service applications interoperate with Web services on many platforms, not just Microsoft platforms, because the applications are one implementation of the SOAP 1.1 or 1.2 and Web Services Description Language (WSDL) 1.1 specifications. An Indigo Web service application can do the following:

- Securely communicate across any number of intermediaries, including firewalls

- Participate in widely distributed transactions

- Create conversations that flow in both directions (that is, services can call clients)

- Provide guaranteed, reliable message delivery

- Support Web service farms for excellent scalability

- Use advanced features such a security, reliability, and transactions with participants that don't use Indigo or Microsoft platforms

- Enable .NET Framework developers to build messaging applications without knowing anything about XML or SOAP

- Enable developers familiar with XML Web services to leverage their XML, WSDL, and SOAP knowledge to work with XML messages described by XSD

- Support easy management of deployed applications

An Indigo Web service application can integrate multiple, diverse participants—each running on different platforms, each separated by public networks, and each using differing security and transaction infrastructures—as components of a single application.

Indigo RemoteObject Service Applications

Indigo RemoteObject service applications provide behavior similar to .NET remoting but with greatly expanded features and support. Both .NET remoting and Indigo RemoteObjects allow client applications to connect with a running object on a server. Both technologies allow client applications to request a server to instantiate a type and then connect to the new instance. Both technologies require the client and the server to possess the type information (metadata) for the remote class.

However, .NET remoting has no authentication or encryption security mechanisms. .NET remoting requires the server to be up and running before any client attempts to connect—there is no automatic activation of the server. .NET remoting also cannot flow a transaction across a remote method call.

However, Indigo RemoteObject applications are built using the Indigo SOAP messaging infrastructure; therefore, they support end-to-end security features, including authentication and encryption, widely distributed and long-running transactions, automatic activation, and a robust management infrastructure, in addition to providing the ability to perform interface-based remoting and use asynchronous server methods.

Choosing Between Indigo Web and RemoteObject Web Services

Both Indigo Web services and Indigo RemoteObject services provide the advanced infrastructure features required for a modern communications application: end-to-end security, distributed transactions, durable messaging, Web farms, and automatic activation. These features simply work regardless of the number of intermediaries between two Indigo applications. Use the criteria shown in Table 6-1 (in descending order of importance) to choose the appropriate type of Indigo service application for your task.

Table 6-1   Criteria for Choosing Indigo Service

Criteria	Indigo Web services	Indigo RemoteObject services
Interoperability with non-Microsoft platforms	✓ Requires the other side of the communication channel to understand SOAP, which is platform agnostic.	✗ Requires Indigo RemoteObject services on both sides of the communication channel.
An improved .NET remoting model	✗	✓ Adds increased support for security, transactions, automatic activation, and ease of management.
Type identity	✗ Accepts structured information and return structured information. Does not maintain type identity.	✓ Preserves the exact type identity of the managed object on both sides of the communication channel.

Programming Web Services

Web services are methods that can be called by any client on any platform that communicates through public network and XML protocols. In this section, I'll show you how to define the Web service by using the Indigo framework. I'll also show you how to generate information that describes the service in a platform-agnostic manner. You typically publish this information so that clients on any platform can use your Web service. Finally, I'll show you how to call the service by using a Indigo client application.

Defining a Web Service

First, we need a Web service that clients can call. You perform the following steps to create a Web service using the Indigo Framework:

1. Define a class with one or more public methods.

2. Apply the *DatagramPortTypeAttribute* to the class.

3. Apply the *ServiceMethodAttribute* to the public methods you want to expose as Web service methods. Note that you can have other methods in the class that aren't exposed to Web service clients.

4. Compile the class into a library assembly.

5. Host the service in a host application.

In the following example, we create the *TimeService* assembly, which contains a single class named *WiseOwl.Time*. The class contains a single Web service method named *GetUtcTimeAndDate*, which returns a string representation of the current Universal Time Coordinate (UTC) time for the specified culture.

```
// TimeService.cs
using System;
using System.Globalization;
using System.MessageBus;
using System.MessageBus.Services;
```

```
namespace WiseOwl {
  [DatagramPortType(Name="Time",
                    Namespace="http://www.wiseowl.com/WebServices")]
  public class Time {
    [ServiceMethod]
    public string GetUtcTimeAndDate(string culture) {
      Console.WriteLine ("Client requested UTC time for culture {0}",
                         culture);
      CultureInfo ci = new CultureInfo (culture);
      return DateTime.UtcNow.ToString ("F", ci);
    }
  }
}
```

Hosting the Web Service

Generally, you will build Web service implementations into one or more library assemblies. You then need a host application that configures the Indigo Framework to listen for requests for that service. When Indigo receives a request for a service, it loads the Web service library, creates an instance of your service class, and calls the appropriate method on the instance.

You need to perform the following two steps to host an Indigo Web service:

1. Call *ServiceEnvironment.Load* to acquire a service environment from a configuration file.

2. Call *ServiceEnvironment.Open* to instruct MessageBus to begin listening for messages to this service.

If you are not using automatic activation, you must keep the application running if you want the service to continue processing messages. When your host application is a Windows Forms application or a Windows Service, the application automatically continues to run until it is explicitly shut down. Therefore, these types of applications typically need to do nothing special to keep the application running. However, as we're using a simple Console application as our host, we call *Console.ReadLine* to block the main thread until the user presses the Enter key to terminate the host application. Thread pool threads will service the Web service requests.

The following example is a generic host application. It hosts all Web services defined in the application's configuration file.

```
// host.cs
using System;
using System.MessageBus;
using System.MessageBus.Services;

class Host {
  static void Main(string[] args) {
    // The service environment needs to be loaded before it can be used.
    // The Load method loads the configuration from the configuration file.
    ServiceEnvironment se = null;
    try {
        se = ServiceEnvironment.Load ();

        // Open the environment to allow client connections
        se.Open ();
        Console.WriteLine("Press enter to stop the services...");
        Console.ReadLine ();
    }
    finally {
      // Must close the environment to cleanup server promptly
      if (se != null) se.Close ();
    }
  }
}
```

The generic host application instructs Indigo to obtain all its configuration information from the application's configuration file. As the host application is named host.exe, the application configuration file should be named host.exe.config and reside in the same directory as host.exe.

There are three main items of interest in this configuration file:

■   The main service environment definition

■   The port *identityRole* element

■   The *activatableServices* child elements

You can define multiple service environments in a configuration file; however, the *ServiceEnvironment.Load* method loads the environment named *main* by default so that's the only one we've defined. We define a port mapped to the URL listed as the value of the *identityRole* element. Clients will use this URL to contact the server. The server will listen for requests addressed to this endpoint. The *activatableServices* element contains a list of the fully qualified types that the Indigo Framework can load and activate when receiving a request for the time. Recall that a fully qualified type name is a string consisting of the namespace-qualified type name, followed by a comma, followed by the full name of the assembly.

We've also included a number of configuration entries to disable security for this simple application. Later in the chapter, I'll discuss communications security in more detail.

```
<configuration>
  <system.messagebus>
    <serviceEnvironments>
      <serviceEnvironment name="main">
        <port>
  <identityRole>soap.tcp://localhost:46000/TimeService/</identityRole>
        </port>
        <!-- CAUTION: Security disabled for demonstration purposes only. -->
        <remove name="securityManager" />
        <policyManager>
          <!-- CAUTION: Security disabled for demonstration purposes only. -->
          <!--
  Permits unsigned policy statements. Default requires signed policy statements -->
          <areUntrustedPolicyAttachmentsAccepted>
            true
          </areUntrustedPolicyAttachmentsAccepted>
          <isPolicyReturned>true</isPolicyReturned>
        </policyManager>
         <serviceManager>
         <activatableServices>
           <add type="WiseOwl.Time, TimeService" />
         </activatableServices>
        </serviceManager>
      </serviceEnvironment>
    </serviceEnvironments>
  </system.messagebus>
</configuration>
```

Obtaining the WSDL for Your Web Service

Now that you have a working Web service, you'd like to create a client that uses the Web service. Before you can write a client that uses the service, you'll need a description of the service. The Web Service Description Language (WSDL) 1.1 and extensions describe a contract that a Web service will uphold. Basically, WSDL allows Web service developers to publish a description of their services in a platform-agnostic manner. Typically, the first step in consuming a Web service is obtaining the WSDL description of the server. You can use the Wsdl-gen.exe utility to produce the WSDL for your Indigo Web services.

To obtain WSDL for a Web Service, run the following command where *<assemblyFileName>* is the assembly containing the service: **wsdlgen <assemblyFileName>**.

In the prior example, I used *"wsdlgen TimeService.dll"*, and it produced two files: a .wsdl file and an .xsd file. The .wsdl file contains the description of the service: the name of the messages accepted by the server, the names of the parts of the messages (for example, the parameters), the port name and type used by the server, and the operations supported on the port.

```
<!-- www_wiseowl_com.WebServices.wsdl -->

<definitions xmlns:s="http://www.w3.org/2001/XMLSchema"
             xmlns:gxa="http://schemas.xmlsoap.org/wsdl/gxa/2003/01/extensions"
             xmlns:i0="http://www.wiseowl.com/WebServices"
             xmlns:tns=http://www.wiseowl.com/WebServices
             targetNamespace="http://www.wiseowl.com/WebServices"
             xmlns="http://schemas.xmlsoap.org/wsdl/">
  <import namespace="http://www.wiseowl.com/WebServices" />
  <types />
  <message name="GetUtcTimeAndDateRequest">
    <part element="tns:GetUtcTimeAndDateRequest" name="parameters" />
  </message>
  <message name="GetUtcTimeAndDateResponse">
    <part element="tns:GetUtcTimeAndDateResponse" name="parameters" />
  </message>
  <portType gxa:correlation="response" name="Time" gxa:usingName="TimeClient">
    <operation name="GetUtcTimeAndDate" gxa:parameterOrder="tns:culture"
                                        gxa:transaction="reject">
      <input message="tns:GetUtcTimeAndDateRequest"
             name="GetUtcTimeAndDateRequest" />
      <output message="tns:GetUtcTimeAndDateResponse"
              name="GetUtcTimeAndDateResponse" />
    </operation>
  </portType>
</definitions>
```

The .xsd file contains the XML schema definition of the messages mentioned in the .wsdl file. Note that the prior .wsdl file described an input message of type *GetUtcTimeAndDateRequest* and an output message of type *GetUtcTimeAndDateResponse*, both in the *http://www.wiseowl.com/WebServices* namespace. The following .xsd file contains the definition of those two XML types.

```
<!-- www_wiseowl_com.WebServices.xsd -->

<?xml version="1.0" encoding="utf-8"?>
<xs:schema xmlns:tns=http://www.wiseowl.com/WebServices
           elementFormDefault="qualified"
           targetNamespace="http://www.wiseowl.com/WebServices"
           xmlns:xs="http://www.w3.org/2001/XMLSchema">
  <xs:element name="GetUtcTimeAndDateRequest">
    <xs:complexType>
      <xs:sequence>
        <xs:element minOccurs="0" name="culture" type="xs:string" />
      </xs:sequence>
    </xs:complexType>
  </xs:element>
  <xs:element name="GetUtcTimeAndDateResponse">
    <xs:complexType>
      <xs:sequence>
        <xs:element minOccurs="0" name="returnValue" type="xs:string" />
      </xs:sequence>
    </xs:complexType>
  </xs:element>
</xs:schema>
```

Because the .wsdl and .xsd files describe your Web service in a platform-agnostic manner, all the information clients need to connect and send requests to your service is contained within those two files. If you publish those files, clients on any platform can, with varying levels of difficulty depending on their tools, create a client for your service.

Creating the Metadata for the Web Service Client

Let's look at the process of creating an Indigo Web service client for an arbitrary Web service. Processing XML directly, in my opinion, is a pain. I don't want to do that. I'd prefer that the framework encapsulate all the details of generating a Web service request, sending it, and parsing the response. In fact, I'd like a managed class that looks and behaves like the actual service to the client but, when used, really sends messages to the actual service. A class is a bit of overkill—an interface would be a better design choice.

Given that you have the .wsdl and .xsd definitions of a Web service, you can use the Wsdlgen.exe tool again to generate a source code file that contains a managed code definition for the Web service. You can then build the source code into an assembly that client code references, or you can include it as a source file in your client application.

Wsdlgen.exe uses .wsdl and .xsd files to create a source code definition of an interface you can use to call the service from a client application.

To create source code describing a Web service, obtain WSDL and any XSD that describes the service with which you want to have a conversation. Run the Wsdlgen utility using the following command:

wsdlgen <WSDL file> <any XSD files>

The following source code was generated by Wsdlgen.exe from the .wsdl and .xsd files that describe the TimeService Web service we previously created. I reformatted the code slightly to make it easier to read.

```
// www_wiseowl_com.WebServices.cs

//------------------------------------------------------------------------------
// <autogenerated>
//     This code was generated by a tool.
//     Runtime Version:1.2.30616.0
//
//     Changes to this file may cause incorrect behavior and will be lost if
//     the code is regenerated.
// </autogenerated>
//------------------------------------------------------------------------------

//
// This source code was auto-generated by WsdlGen, Version=1.2.30616.0.
//
using System.MessageBus.Services;

namespace www_wiseowl_com.WebServices {
  [DatagramPortType( Namespace="http://www.wiseowl.com/WebServices")]
  public interface ITime {
      [ServiceMethod]
      string GetUtcTimeAndDate(string culture);
  }

  [PortTypeChannel(Namespace="http://www.wiseowl.com/WebServices")]
  public interface ITimeChannel : IDatagramPortTypeChannel {
    [WrappedMessage(Namespace="http://www.wiseowl.com/WebServices")]
    [ServiceMethod]
    [return: WrappedMessage(Namespace="http://www.wiseowl.com/WebServices")]
    string GetUtcTimeAndDate(string culture);
  }
}
```

The prior source file has two noteworthy aspects. The Wsdlgen tool defines an interface, named *ITime*, that contains each service method implemented by the Web service. It also defines an interface, named *ITimeChannel*, which is the strongly typed channel you use when communicating with the Web service.

Calling the Web Service from a Client

To use these interfaces in a client application, your client application must do the following:

- Call *ServiceEnvironment.Load* to acquire the default service environment from a configuration file.

- Extract the *ServiceManager* object from the *ServiceEnvironment*.

- Use the *ServiceManager.CreateChannel* method to create the channel interface that can connect to the Web service.

- Reference the definition of the channel interface you produced using the Wsdlgen tool.

The following code is a client that uses the Time Web service:

```
// client.cs
using System;
using System.MessageBus;
using System.MessageBus.Services;
using www_wiseowl_com.WebServices;  // The imported service namespace

public class Client {
  public static void Main(string[] args) {
    string culture = "en-US";
    if (args.Length > 0) culture = args[0];

    // Load the default service environment, called "main".
    ServiceEnvironment se = null;

    try {
      se = ServiceEnvironment.Load();

      // Retrieve the ServiceManager from the default environment
      ServiceManager sm =
        se[typeof(ServiceManager)] as ServiceManager;
      if (sm == null)
        throw new Exception ("ServiceManager is not available.");

      // Start the service environment.
      se.Open();

      // Create a proxy channel that points to the service to call.
      Uri uri = new Uri("soap.tcp://localhost:46000/TimeService/");
      ITimeChannel channel = (ITimeChannel)
        sm.CreateChannel(typeof(ITimeChannel), uri);
```

```
      Console.WriteLine(channel.GetUtcTimeAndDate (culture));
    }
    catch (Exception e) {
      Console.WriteLine (e);
    }
    finally {
      if (se != null) se.Close();
    }
  }
}
```

As with the Web service itself, the client application can obtain its Indigo configuration information by asking the Framework to load the information from the application configuration file. I named the client application client.exe, so here is its associated client.exe.config configuration file.

```
<configuration>
  <system.messagebus>
    <serviceEnvironments>
      <serviceEnvironment name="main">
        <port>
          <identityRole>soap.tcp://localhost:46001/TimeClient/</identityRole>
        </port>
        <!-- CAUTION: Security disabled for demonstration purposes only. -->
        <remove name="securityManager" />
        <policyManager>
          <!-- CAUTION: Security disabled for demonstration purposes only. -->
          <!--
Permits unsigned policy statements. Default requires signed policy statements -->
          <areUntrustedPolicyAttachmentsAccepted>
            true
          </areUntrustedPolicyAttachmentsAccepted>
          <isPolicyReturned>true</isPolicyReturned>
        </policyManager>
      </serviceEnvironment>
    </serviceEnvironments>
  </system.messagebus>
</configuration>
```

Note that I define a port and an identify role for the client. The *identity-Role* element's value must be a unique identifier and allow a service to initiate communications with the client. In my example, I specify both the name and location of the client, which eliminates the need to specify available transports separately. Regardless, my client application doesn't use this server-callback capability.

Programmatic Configuration

I think placing most communications configuration information in a separate file from the application is the best approach for most scenarios. However, occasionally you might not know until runtime which service you want, or you might want to determine other configuration parameters dynamically. Indigo allows you to configure the runtime environment programmatically—in fact, loading the configuration file really just causes the runtime itself to issue these programmatic requests.

The code is fairly self-explanatory, so I'll simply list the source for the programmatic versions of the Web service and client. Note that these changes don't affect the service itself; all the changes occur in the service's host application. Here's the source code for the host:

```
// host.cs
using System;
using System.Authorization;
using System.MessageBus;
using System.MessageBus.Policy;
using System.MessageBus.Security;
using System.MessageBus.Services;

class Host {
  static void Main(string[] args) {
    // Load and configure the default ServiceEnvironment.
    ServiceEnvironment se = null;
    try {
      se = ServiceEnvironment.Load();
      Port port = se [typeof(Port)] as Port;
      port.IdentityRole = new Uri("soap.tcp://localhost:46000/TimeService/");

      // Register the Time type as activatable.
      ServiceManager sm = se [typeof(ServiceManager)] as ServiceManager;
      sm.ActivatableServices.Add(typeof(WiseOwl.Time));

      // Enable the PolicyManager to accept unsigned policy messages
      // because this service does not have X509 certificates.
      // For demonstration purposes only.
      PolicyManager pm = se[typeof(PolicyManager)] as PolicyManager;
      pm.AreUntrustedPolicyAttachmentsAccepted = true;
      pm.IsPolicyReturned = true;

      // Disable security for receiving messages.
      // For demonstration purposes only.
      SecurityManager secman = (SecurityManager)se[typeof(SecurityManager)];
      secman.IsEnabledForReceive = false;
```

```
      se.Open();
      Console.WriteLine("Press enter to stop the services...");
      Console.ReadLine();
    }
    finally {
      if (se != null) se.Close();
    }
  }
}
```

And here's the source code for the client:

```
// client.cs
using System;
using System.Authorization;
using System.MessageBus;
using System.MessageBus.Policy;
using System.MessageBus.Security;
using System.MessageBus.Services;
using www_wiseowl_com.WebServices;  // The imported service namespace

public class Client {
  public static void Main(string[] args) {
    string culture = "en-US";
    if (args.Length > 0) culture = args[0];

    // Load the default service environment, called "main".
    ServiceEnvironment se = null;

    try {
      se = ServiceEnvironment.Load();

      // Retrieve the ServiceManager from the default environment
      ServiceManager sm =
        se [typeof(ServiceManager)] as ServiceManager;
      if (sm == null)
        throw new Exception ("ServiceManager is not available.");

      // Start the service environment programmatically.
      Port port = se[typeof(Port)] as Port;
      port.IdentityRole = new Uri("soap.tcp://localhost:46001/TimeClient/");

      // Allow PolicyManager to accept unsigned policy messages because
      // client does not have X509 certificates.
      // CAUTION: Security disabled for demonstration purposes.
      PolicyManager pm = se[typeof(PolicyManager)] as PolicyManager;
      pm.AreUntrustedPolicyAttachmentsAccepted = true;
      pm.IsPolicyReturned = true;
```

```
          // Turn off access control.
          // CAUTION: Security disabled for demonstration purposes.
          SecurityManager secman = (SecurityManager) se[typeof(SecurityManager)];
        secman.DefaultReceiverScope.AccessControl.AccessRequirementChoices.Add
                                          (new AccessRequirementChoice());
          secman.IsEnabledForReceive = false;

          // Start the service environment.
          se.Open();

          // Create a proxy channel that points to the service to call.
          Uri uri = new Uri("soap.tcp://localhost:46000/TimeService/");
          ITimeChannel channel = (ITimeChannel)
              sm.CreateChannel(typeof(ITimeChannel), uri);

          Console.WriteLine(channel.GetUtcTimeAndDate (culture));
        }
        catch (Exception e) {
          Console.WriteLine (e);
        }
        finally {
          if (se != null) se.Close();
        }
      }
    }
```

Programming Remote Objects

You can use RemoteObjects in two ways. You can create a new instance of a remote object. You can also obtain a proxy to an existing remote object so that you can invoke its methods. RemoteObjects provide communications functionality to programs running in separate application domains in the same Win32 process, running in different processes on the same machine, or even running across machines over the Internet.

From the server's point of view, there are two aspects to serving a remote object. You can publish the ability to create a new instance of a remote object class, or you can publish the ability to connect to an existing instance of a remote object class. Either way, you need a remote object class, so let's start there.

Creating a *TimeZone* RemoteObject

It's actually easier to define a class that supports Indigo RemoteObjects than it is to define a Web service class. A RemoteObject must derive directly or indirectly from *System.MarshalByRefObject*. Note that .NET remoting had the same base class requirement, so a class written to be used by .NET remoting can generally be used as an Indigo RemoteObject.

The following code example creates a *TimeZoneObject* RemoteObject that has public methods that return time and date information. I'll be using this class in the rest of the examples in this section. A client creates a *TimeZoneObject* instance for a specific time zone. The *GetCurrentTimeAndDate* method for that instance then returns the current time in the specified time zone.

```csharp
using System;
using System.Globalization;

public class TimeZoneObject : MarshalByRefObject {
  private Guid      myID = Guid.NewGuid ();
  private TimeSpan myOffset;

  public TimeZoneObject (string tz) {
    myOffset = ConvertZoneToUtcOffset (tz);
    Console.WriteLine("Creating object {0} for zone {1}", myID, tz);
  }

  public string GetCurrentTimeAndDate (CultureInfo ci) {
    if (ci == null) ci = new CultureInfo ("");
    Console.WriteLine("{0} returning current time/date for culture {1}",
                  myID, ci.ToString());
    return (DateTime.UtcNow + myOffset).ToString ("F", ci);
  }

  public string GetUtcTimeAndDate (CultureInfo ci) {
    return DateTime.UtcNow.ToString ("F", ci);
  }

  private TimeSpan ConvertZoneToUtcOffset (string tz) {
    string upperTZ = tz.ToUpper();
    switch (upperTZ) {
      case "ADT":                       // Atlantic Daylight -3 hours
        return new TimeSpan (-3, 0, 0);
      case "AST":                       // Atlantic Standard
      case "EDT":                       // Eastern Daylight  -4 hours
        return new TimeSpan (-4, 0, 0);
      case "EST":                       // Eastern Standard
      case "CDT":                       // Central Daylight  -5 hours
        return new TimeSpan (-5, 0, 0);
      case "CST":                       // Central Standard
      case "MDT":                       // Mountain Daylight -6 hours
        return new TimeSpan (-6, 0, 0);
      case "MST":                       // Mountain Standard
```

```
        case "PDT":                          // Pacific Daylight -7 hours
            return new TimeSpan (-7, 0, 0);
        case "PST":                          // Pacific Standard
//case "ADT":                                // Alaskan Daylight -8 hours
            return new TimeSpan (-8, 0, 0);
        case "ALA":                          // Alaskan Standard -9 hours
            return new TimeSpan (-9, 0, 0);
        case "HAW":                          // Hawaiian Standard -10 hours
            return new TimeSpan (-10, 0, 0);
        case "UTC":
        case "GMT":
        case "ZULU":                         // So it's not a real zone name
            return new TimeSpan (0, 0, 0);
        case "CET":                          // Central European
        case "FWT":                          // French Winter
        case "MET":                          // Middle European
        case "MEWT":                         // Middle European Winter
        case "SWT":                          // Swedish Winter  +1 hour
            return new TimeSpan (+1, 0, 0);
        case "EET":                          // Eastern European, USSR Zone 1 +2
            return new TimeSpan (+2, 0, 0);
        case "BT":                           // Baghdad, USSR Zone 2 +3 hours
            return new TimeSpan (+3, 0, 0);
        case "ZP4":                          // USSR Zone 3 +4 hours
            return new TimeSpan (+4, 0, 0);
        case "ZP5":                          // USSR Zone 4 +5 hours
            return new TimeSpan (+5, 0, 0);
        case "ZP6":                          // USSR Zone 5 +6 hours
            return new TimeSpan (+6, 0, 0);
        case "WAST":                         // West Australian Standard +7 hours
            return new TimeSpan (+7, 0, 0);
        case "CCT":                          // China Coast, USSR Zone 7 +8
            return new TimeSpan (+8, 0, 0);
        case "JST":                          // Japan Standard, USSR Zone 8 +9
            return new TimeSpan (+9, 0, 0);
        case "EAST":                         // East Australian Standard GST
        case "Guam":                         // Standard, USSR Zone 9  +10 hours
            return new TimeSpan (+10, 0, 0);
        case "IDLE":                         // International Date Line
        case "NZST":                         // New Zealand Standard
        case "NZT":                          // New Zealand
            return new TimeSpan (+12, 0, 0);
        default:
            throw new Exception ("Unrecognized time zone");
        }
    }
}
```

Hosting a RemoteObject Class

In your RemoteObject hosting application, just like the Web service, you create a *ServiceEnvironment* object by loading an application configuration file and passing the name of the service environment configuration settings that you want to use. As before, I'll default to loading the main service environment from the configuration file.

```
using System;
using System.MessageBus;
using System.MessageBus.Remoting;

class Host {
  static void Main () {
    ServiceEnvironment se = null;

    try {
        se = ServiceEnvironment.Load ();
        RemotingManager rm = se[typeof(RemotingManager)] as RemotingManager;
        if (rm == null)
            throw new Exception("No RemotingManager in ServiceEnvironment.");

        // Start the ServiceEnvironment.
        se.Open ();

        // Register an instance of a TimeZoneObject for
        // remote connection hosted in this service environment.
        TimeZoneObject tzoPST = new TimeZoneObject ("PST");
        TimeZoneObject tzoHAW = new TimeZoneObject ("HAW");
        TimeZoneObject tzoCET = new TimeZoneObject ("CET");
        TimeZoneObject tzoGMT = new TimeZoneObject ("GMT");

        // A client can create a proxy to a published object using
        // RemotingManager.GetObject
        PublishedServerObject psoPST =
            new PublishedServerObject (tzoPST, new Uri("urn:PST"));
        rm.PublishedServerObjects.Add (psoPST);

        PublishedServerObject psoHAW =
            new PublishedServerObject (tzoHAW, new Uri("urn:HAW"));
        rm.PublishedServerObjects.Add (psoHAW);

        PublishedServerObject psoCET =
            new PublishedServerObject (tzoCET, new Uri("urn:CET"));
        rm.PublishedServerObjects.Add (psoCET);

        PublishedServerObject psoGMT =
            new PublishedServerObject (tzoGMT, new Uri("urn:GMT"));
        rm.PublishedServerObjects.Add (psoGMT);
```

```
        Console.WriteLine("Listening for requests. Press Enter to exit...");
        Console.ReadLine();

        // Cancel the publication of the objects.
        rm.PublishedServerObjects.Remove(psoPST);
        rm.PublishedServerObjects.Remove(psoHAW);
        rm.PublishedServerObjects.Remove(psoCET);
        rm.PublishedServerObjects.Remove(psoGMT);
    }
    finally {
        if (se != null) se.Close();
    }
  }
}
```

Note that in a RemoteObject hosting application, I use the *Remoting-Manager* class instead of the *ServiceManager*, as I did in my Web service. The unique part of this example is my use of the *RemotingManager* to publish objects the hosting application has created and initialized. I create a few *Time-ZoneObject* instances as usual:

```
TimeZoneObject tzoPST = new TimeZoneObject ("PST");
. . .
TimeZoneObject tzoGMT = new TimeZoneObject ("GMT");
```

However, I then publish the objects by creating a set of *PublishedServer-Object* instances, each one of which associates a particular *TimeZoneObject* object with a unique name. When I add the *PublishedServerObject* instances to the *RemotingManager PublishedServerObjects* collection, the *RemotingManager* allows clients to access each published object by its unique name.

```
PublishedServerObject psoPST =
    new PublishedServerObject (tzoPST, new Uri("urn:PST"));
rm.PublishedServerObjects.Add (psoPST);
```

I also have, by now, the expected configuration file for the server. The only difference between this RemoteObject configuration file and the earlier Web service configuration file is that I've specified a different port identity.

```
<configuration>
  <system.messagebus>
    <serviceEnvironments>
      <serviceEnvironment name="main">
        <port>
          <identityRole>
            soap.tcp://localhost:46010/TimeZoneObjects
          </identityRole>
        </port>
```

```
<!-- CAUTION: Security disabled for demonstration purposes only. -->
<remove name="securityManager" />
<policyManager>
  <!-- CAUTION: Security disabled for demonstration purposes only. -->
  <!--
Permits unsigned policy statements. Default requires signed policy statements -->
  <areUntrustedPolicyAttachmentsAccepted>
    true
  </areUntrustedPolicyAttachmentsAccepted>
  <isPolicyReturned>true</isPolicyReturned>
</policyManager>
<remotingManager>
</remotingManager>
    </serviceEnvironment>
  </serviceEnvironments>
</system.messagebus>
</configuration>
```

Connecting to a Remote Instance of a RemoteObject

A client application can connect to a published RemoteObject by

■   Creating the *ServiceEnvironment* by calling the *Load* method as usual

■   Obtaining a *RemotingManager* from the *ServiceEnvironment*

■   Opening the *ServiceEnvironment*

■   Creating a URI that addresses the desired *RemotingObject* server

■   Calling the *RemotingManager GetObject* method and specifying the server's URI and the unique name of the specific object to which you want to connect

■   Calling methods, access fields, and properties on the remote object

The following *RemotingObject* client application connects to a published *TimeZoneObject* and retrieves and displays the current time in that time zone.

```
using System;
using System.Globalization;
using System.MessageBus;
using System.MessageBus.Remoting;

class Client {
  static void Main (string[] args) {
    string zone = "PST";
    if (args.Length > 0 && args[0].Length > 0) zone = args[0];
```

```
CultureInfo ci = new CultureInfo ("");
if (args.Length > 1 && args[1].Length > 0) ci = new CultureInfo (args[1]);

ServiceEnvironment se = null;

try {
   se = ServiceEnvironment.Load ();
   RemotingManager rm = se[typeof(RemotingManager)] as RemotingManager;
   if (rm == null)
    throw new Exception("No RemotingManager in ServiceEnvironment.");

   // Start the ServiceEnvironment.
   se.Open();

   Uri serverPortUri =
       new Uri("soap.tcp://localhost:46010/TimeZoneObjects");

   // Build a proxy to an existing object
   string urn = "urn:" + zone;
   TimeZoneObject tzo =
       rm.GetObject (serverPortUri, new Uri(urn)) as TimeZoneObject;

   if (tzo != null) {
     Console.WriteLine ("It is currently {0} in the {1} time zone.",
                        tzo.GetCurrentTimeAndDate (ci), zone);
   }
   else {
     Console.WriteLine ("Could not connect to the remote object.");
   }
 }
 finally {
   if (se != null) se.Close();
 }
 }
}
```

Allowing Clients to Create a New Instance of a RemoteObject

A RemoteObject host application can also allow client applications to create their very own personal, private instances of a hosted class. In this case, the hosting application is typically extremely simple. It simply loads the configuration file in which all the real information resides.

```
using System;
using System.MessageBus;
using System.MessageBus.Remoting;
```

```
class Host {
  static void Main() {
    ServiceEnvironment se = null;

    try {
      se = ServiceEnvironment.Load ();
      se.Open ();

      Console.WriteLine ("Listening for requests. Press Enter to exit...");
      Console.ReadLine ();
    }
    finally {
      if (se != null) se.Close ();
    }
  }
}
```

A configuration file that allows clients to create new instances of types contains a *publishedServerTypes* element. Each *publishedServerTypes* element's child *add* element lists a fully qualified type that client applications can request the server to create.

```
<configuration>
  <system.messagebus>
    <serviceEnvironments>
      <serviceEnvironment name="main">
        <port>
          <identityRole>
            soap.tcp://localhost:46010/TimeZoneObjects
          </identityRole>
        </port>
        <!-- CAUTION: Security disabled for demonstration purposes only. -->
        <remove name="securityManager" />
        <policyManager>
          <!-- CAUTION: Security disabled for demonstration purposes only. -->
          <!--
Permits unsigned policy statements. Default requires signed policy statements -->
          <areUntrustedPolicyAttachmentsAccepted>
            true
          </areUntrustedPolicyAttachmentsAccepted>
          <isPolicyReturned>true</isPolicyReturned>
        </policyManager>
        <remotingManager>
          <publishedServerTypes>
            <add type="TimeZoneObject, TimeZoneObject"/>
          </publishedServerTypes>
```

```
        </remotingManager>
      </serviceEnvironment>
    </serviceEnvironments>
  </system.messagebus>
</configuration>
```

Creating a New Instance of a RemoteObject

A client application can also create its very own personal, private instance of a remote class using the *RemotingManager*. The host application in this case is extremely simple:

- Creating the *ServiceEnvironment* by calling the *Load* method as usual

- Obtaining a *RemotingManager* from the *ServiceEnvironment*

- Opening the *ServiceEnvironment*

- Creating a URI that addresses the desired *RemotingObject* server

- Calling the *RemotingManager GetObject* method and specifying the server's URI and the unique name of the specific object to which you want to connect

- Calling methods, access fields, and properties on the remote object

The following *RemotingObject* client application connects to a published *TimeZoneObject* and retrieves and displays the current time in that time zone.

```
using System;
using System.Globalization;
using System.MessageBus;
using System.MessageBus.Remoting;

class Client {
  static void Main (string[] args) {
    string zone = "PST";
    if (args.Length > 0 && args[0].Length > 0) zone = args[0];

    CultureInfo ci = new CultureInfo ("");
    if (args.Length > 1 && args[1].Length > 0) ci = new CultureInfo (args[1]);

    ServiceEnvironment se = null;

    try {
      se = ServiceEnvironment.Load ();
      RemotingManager rm = se[typeof(RemotingManager)] as RemotingManager;
      if (rm == null)
        throw new Exception("No RemotingManager in ServiceEnvironment.");
```

```
    // Start the ServiceEnvironment.
    se.Open();

    Uri serverPortUri =
        new Uri("soap.tcp://localhost:46010/TimeZoneObjects");

    // Build a proxy to an existing object
    string urn = "urn:" + zone;
    TimeZoneObject tzo =
        rm.GetObject (serverPortUri, new Uri(urn)) as TimeZoneObject;

    if (tzo != null) {
      Console.WriteLine ("It is currently {0} in the {1} time zone.",
                          tzo.GetCurrentTimeAndDate (ci), zone);
    }
    else {
      Console.WriteLine ("Could not connect to the remote object.");
    }
  }
  finally {
    if (se != null) se.Close();
  }
 }
}
```

Securing Indigo Applications

One major improvement in Indigo applications as compared to prior managed-communications technologies is that Indigo applications allow you to create secure communications. Indigo provides common security services such as confidentiality (also known as encryption), integrity, authentication, and authorization. By default, the Indigo performs many security tasks (such as encryption and digital signing) for you, greatly easing the job of building a secure application.

Effectively securing your Indigo application primarily consists of the following steps:

1. Securing access to the methods your application publishes or exposes.

2. Securing the content of messages sent to and from nodes of your application.

Let's look at securing access to published methods. Often you need to restrict access to your Indigo application to only a select group of predefined users. To do so, Indigo must determine the identity of a client using an authentication service. Indigo provides the following built-in authentication services:

- Microsoft Windows authentication
- X.509 certificate authentication
- Basic user name and password authentication

When writing an application, the developer determines which roles can access a method. When deploying a Message Bus application, an administrator assigns user and group memberships to one or more roles. When Indigo authenticates a client, it determines the client's identity and maps that identity to a role.

An Indigo application might need to communicate across a network where anyone can monitor the messages. In many applications, you will not want third parties to read the messages during transmission or to alter or replace messages during transmission. You can use encryption to protect the confidentiality of your messages. Indigo supports encryption using both symmetric and asymmetric algorithms. Similarly, you can use digital signatures to protect the integrity of your messages and to verify the authenticity of the message sender.

Indigo provides most of the security you need by default. Message Bus applications automatically adapt to meet the security requirements specified by receiving nodes as defined by the WS-SecurityPolicy specification. For example, if you write a client and use the default configuration schemes, your client will automatically conform to the encryption and authentication requirements of most servers to which it might connect. In many cases, security requirements need to be explicitly specified only on the server side. Indigo provides many default security schemes that you can easily control through code attributes and configuration.

The Indigo security system automatically implements most security details when you add security attributes to your communications methods. For example, when you need to encrypt a message, you specify that you want to perform encryption by decorating your methods with descriptive attributes. When the method is accessed, Indigo automatically encrypts the message for you. You request Web method access control similarly.

Indigo provides two mechanisms to define and modify security requirements. A developer can define security requirements in a configuration file or explicitly in code, similar to the way you can define the communications transports and ports in a configuration file or code. However, system administrators might also want to define or modify the security requirements for a deployed application. They would use the configuration files to specify the new requirements.

Security Manager

The *SecurityManager* is the primary component of the Indigo security system. It defines the security requirements that are applied to incoming and outgoing messages of a specified port. Typically, every port has one *SecurityManager*.

You can easily create a new *SecurityManager* automatically when you create a new *ServiceEnvironment*. When you create a *ServiceEnvironment* by loading a configuration file, the Indigo framework automatically creates a *SecurityManager* if a definition of a *SecurityManager* is present in the configuration file. The *SecurityManager* contains three important properties: *Scopes*, *Bindings*, and *EndpointSettings*.

Scopes Property

The *Scopes* property contains a collection of security scope objects.

Security Scope

A security scope defines the security requirements you want associated with a service method. For example, if you want to specify that a method needs to use encryption, you would define it in a security scope. If you want to specify that a method requires an access check, you would also define it in a security scope.

You use a security scope to specify the following requirements for a Web service method:

- It must encrypt its message bodies.

- It requires an access check (and that implicitly involves message integrity and sender authentication)

Security Profile

A security profile defines how to implement a security requirement. It specifies how the encryption, integrity and sender authentication requirements can be met. For example, most systems support a variety of encryption algorithms. One security profile can specify that the DES3 encryption should be used, while a different profile specifies RSA encryption.

The following security requirement implementations can be defined using security profiles:

- Algorithms to use for encryption

- Keys or X.509 certificates to use for encryption

- The type of authentication to use (such as Windows, basic user name and password, or X.509 certificate authorization)

- How to use licensing

Bindings Property

Security scopes are not associated with a security profile until the two are explicitly bound by a security binding. Generally, your application will have one or more scopes associated with every service method or remote object. A system will typically have numerous profiles available. When an administrator configures or deploys an application, the administrator decides which implementation—for example, authentication type—to use by binding a scope to a profile. The *SecurityManager Bindings* property contains these bindings and is populated by configuration information in the Machine.config and Application.config files when you create a new *SecurityManager*.

EndpointSettings Property

The *EndpointSettings* property encapsulates security capabilities of the current endpoint. All cryptographic algorithms, keys, X.509 certificates, and authentication providers are enumerated here. Like the *Bindings* property, the *Endpoint-Settings* property is typically populated by information from Machine.config and Application.config files when you create a new *SecurityManager*. These values are usually configured during application deployment and administration rather than during development.

Design-Time vs. Deploy-Time

While this design initially seems complicated, the distinction between security scopes and security profiles allow you to separate your security requirements from your security implementation. Typically, you will specify your security requirements in code (for example, this method restricts access control to users in role X). However, you typically specify the implementation of that security requirement in a configuration file (for example, that Windows authentication should be used). This separation allows you to change the implementation of a security requirement (type of authentication, type of encryption, and so forth) that your application uses without having to recompile.

Creating an Authenticated Web Service

Let's add authentication to my original Web service example from this chapter. In the following example, I've simply added the two lines in bold: a *using* declaration, and a *ServiceSecurity* attribute that indicates Indigo should secure access to the *GetUtcTimeAndDate* method.

```
using System;
using System.Globalization;
using System.MessageBus;
using System.MessageBus.Services;
```

```
using System.MessageBus.Security;

namespace WiseOwl {
  [DatagramPortType(Name="Time",
                    Namespace="http://www.wiseowl.com/WebServices")]
  public class Time {
    [ServiceSecurity(Name="GetUtcDateAndTimeScope", Role="StandardUserRole")]
    [ServiceMethod]
    public string GetUtcTimeAndDate(string culture) {
      Console.WriteLine ("Client requested UTC time for culture {0}", culture);
      CultureInfo ci = new CultureInfo (culture);
      return DateTime.UtcNow.ToString ("F", ci);
    }
  }
}
```

I didn't change the host application at all, so I won't list it again here. However, I did add a *securityManager* element to the host's application configuration file, host.exe.config. Note that the *securityManager* element contains an *applicationSecurity* element with a binding that maps the scope named "*GetUtcDateAndTimeScope*" to the profile named "*windows*".

```
<configuration>
  <system.messagebus>
    <serviceEnvironments>
      <serviceEnvironment name="main">
        <port>
          <identityRole>soap.tcp://localhost:46000/TimeService/</identityRole>
        </port>
        <!--
Bind the scope defined using ServiceSecurityAttribute to a profile that uses
Windows Authentication. -->
        <securityManager>
          <applicationSecurity>
            <binding scope="GetUtcDateAndTimeScope" profile="windows" />
          </applicationSecurity>
        </securityManager>
        <policyManager>
          <!-- CAUTION: Security disabled for demonstration purposes only. -->
          <!--
Permits unsigned policy statements. Default requires signed policy statements -->
          <areUntrustedPolicyAttachmentsAccepted>
            true
          </areUntrustedPolicyAttachmentsAccepted>
          <isPolicyReturned>true</isPolicyReturned>
        </policyManager>
        <serviceManager>
```

```
    <activatableServices>
      <add type="WiseOwl.Time, TimeService" />
    </activatableServices>
  </serviceManager>
</serviceEnvironment>
</serviceEnvironments>
</system.messagebus>
</configuration>
```

The *ServiceSecurity* attribute on my Web service method states that access to the method is constrained by the scope named *GetUtcDateAndTimeScope*. Conceptually, an administrator has bound that scope name to the *"windows"* profile—a system-defined profile that specifies that the desired implementation is the Windows authentication implementation.

Indigo will now require a client to authenticate using Windows authentication. The method's *ServiceSecurity* attribute requires the authenticated user to be in the role named *StandardUserRole* to access the method. The mapping between users and roles resides in the application's security configuration file, which in this example, is named host.exe.security. In my WiseOwl domain, I've created a new group named *"Indigo Users"* and added my user account to that group. Then in the application's security configuration file, I specify that an authenticated user in the Indigo Users group is in the *StandardUserRole* role and, therefore, has access to my Web service method.

```
<securityData>
  <authorizationData>
    <memoryMapping id="mainAuthorizationData">
      <globalEntries>
        <windowsRoleAssignment domain="WiseOwl" group="Indigo Users"
                    roles = "StandardUserRole"/>
      </globalEntries>
    </memoryMapping>
  </authorizationData>
</securityData>
```

Calling an Authenticated Web Service Method

You can use the original Web service client listed previously in this chapter to call the authenticated version of the Web service method. Run the client while logged in using an account that is currently authenticated by the domain that the Web service recognizes. You don't need to make any changes to the client code to call an authenticated Web service. However, I did need to make one small change to the client's configuration file. The original version removed the security manager from the service environment as follows:

```
<remove name="securityManager" />
```

Now I need the default security manager in the service environment, so I deleted the preceding line from the client.exe.config file for my authenticated Web service client.

Variations on Authentication

Now that I've enabled authentication for my Web service method, I can easily change the type and manner of authentication by editing the configuration files. For example, if I want to switch from Windows authentication to requiring a user name and password, I need to make only two changes at the server and one at the client. First, I change the *securityManager* in my host.exe.config application configuration file so that my security code now binds to the standard *userNamePassword* profile as follows:

```
<securityManager>
  <applicationSecurity>
    <binding scope="GetUtcDateAndTimeScope" profile="userNamePassword" />
  </applicationSecurity>
</securityManager>
```

Then I change my application security file, host.exe.security, so that it specifies the allowed user names and their respective passwords, and maps the user names to the appropriate roles.

```
<securityData>
  <credentials>
    <username id="mainUsers" nonceLength="24">
      <memoryPasswordResolver>
        <add user="Brent" password="password1" />
        <add user="Lisa" password="password2" />
      </memoryPasswordResolver>
    </username>
  </credentials>
  <authorizationData>
    <memoryMapping id="mainAuthorizationData">
      <globalEntries>
        <userNameRoleAssignment user="Brent" roles = "StandardUserRole"/>
        <userNameRoleAssignment user="Lisa" roles = "StandardUserRole"/>
      </globalEntries>
    </memoryMapping>
  </authorizationData>
</securityData>
```

I feel obliged to point out that you can replace the *memoryPassword-Resolver* used in the prior example with your own custom mechanism to retrieve user names and passwords from some more secure and presumably encrypted source.

Because the service application requires a user name and password, I must now change the client application so that it provides the user name and password. The easiest way is to use my original client application and specify the user name and password in the client application's security configuration file. Here's the original client application. The following code is a client application:

```
// client.cs
using System;
using System.MessageBus;
using System.MessageBus.Services;
using www_wiseowl_com.WebServices;   // The imported service namespace

public class Client {
  public static void Main(string[] args) {
    string culture = "en-US";
    if (args.Length > 0) culture = args[0];

    // Load the default service environment, called "main".
    ServiceEnvironment se = null;

    try {
      se = ServiceEnvironment.Load();

      // Retrieve the ServiceManager from the default environment
      ServiceManager sm =
        se[typeof(ServiceManager)] as ServiceManager;
      if (sm == null)
        throw new Exception ("ServiceManager is not available.");

      // Start the service environment.
      se.Open();

      // Create a proxy channel that points to the service to call.
      Uri uri = new Uri("soap.tcp://localhost:46000/TimeService/");
      ITimeChannel channel = (ITimeChannel)
          sm.CreateChannel(typeof(ITimeChannel), uri);

      Console.WriteLine(channel.GetUtcTimeAndDate (culture));
    }
    catch (Exception e) {
      Console.WriteLine (e);
    }
    finally {
      if (se != null) se.Close();
    }
  }
}
```

Because the prior client application loads its configuration from the default service environment, I can specify my security settings using a security configuration file. My client application is named client.exe—therefore my client application security file is client.exe.security and looks like this:

```
<securityData>
    <tokens>
        <tokenCache id="mainTokenCache">
            <userNameToken user="Brent" password="password"/>
            <userNameToken user="Lisa" password="wordpass"/>
        </tokenCache>
    </tokens>
</securityData>
```

Rather than specifying the user name and password pairs in the configuration file, I can alternatively initialize the security token cache programmatically before I open the security environment:

```
// Retrieve the SecurityManager from the default environment
SecurityManager secMan = se [typeof(SecurityManager)] as SecurityManager;

if (secMan == null) {
  throw new ApplicationException("Security Manager not present.");
}
⋮
// Create a new UserName Token and add password and user information.
UserNameToken t = new UserNameToken (userName, password, 24);
secMan.EndpointSettings.TokenCache.AddToken(t);
⋮
se.Open ();
```

Message Confidentiality

When you enable confidentiality on a Web service method, Indigo encrypts the body of your messages automatically. When a client calls your encrypted Web service, Indigo automatically acquires the appropriate keys and encrypts the messages to meet the requirements of the service. An administrator typically decides encryption requirements during deployment by using configuration files.

You enable confidentiality by passing the true *Confidentiality* property of the *ServiceSecurityAttribute*. Therefore, using following attribute in place of the one listed previously requires authentication and authorization to access the method. It also encrypts the SOAP message body of the message sent to the method.

```
[ServiceSecurity(Name="GetUtcDateAndTimeScope",
             Role="StandardUserRole", Confidentiality = true)]
```

As with the prior example, you typically select the specific encryption implementation using configuration file entries.

Reliable and Durable Messaging

Reliable messaging helps protect an application from transient communications problems between nodes by automatic failure detection and transient failure recovery. Indigo normally hides these recoverable errors from your application, allowing you to concentrate on developing your functionality rather than writing lots of code to deal with network reliability issues. Reliable messaging provides certain assurances about the delivery of messages to the applications, and it either fulfills the assurances or informs the application it was unable to fulfill them.

Durable messaging addresses a different problem. Durable messaging insulates applications from node failures at the messaging endpoints that are hosting the application by providing durable storage at the messaging endpoints. This allows Indigo to restore a communications session between messaging endpoints after a failure.

A *dialog* is the key Indigo abstraction that provides reliable message-based communication between Indigo services and other application endpoints. A dialog is a reliable, bi-directional, session-oriented message exchange between two endpoints and essentially consists of the state at these two endpoints. Dialogs can be configured to provide a variety of communication requirements, from a tightly coupled, exactly once, in-order delivery to a more loosely coupled, asynchronous style of delivery.

Reliable messaging between two endpoints requires that each of the endpoints store information about the state of the dialog between them. Indigo stores the state of a dialog in a dialog store at each endpoint. The store allows the objects representing that state to disappear and Indigo can recover the dialog. A durable store provides the ability to recover the dialog. When either the client or the server process that hosts the dialog terminates, it can come back at a later time and continue the dialog from where it left off. Durable storage of dialog state thus makes recovery from process or node failure possible. When the storage is not durable, the objects representing the dialog state are retained only in memory and the dialog will be lost in the event of node failure.

A *dialog channel* provides the delivery assurances for each endpoint of the dialog. This interface provides state management at each dialog endpoint and the methods to manage messages in the send and receive buffers.

Defining a Dialog-Based Service

I need to make only one major change to the previous service application for it to operate using a dialog. Instead of applying the *DatagramPortTypeAttribute* to the Web service class, I need to apply the *DialogPortTypeAttribute* to the class, as shown in the following example. The *DialogPortTypeAttribute* requests Indigo to establish a session between an instance of this service class and the client who created it. All subsequent communication from and to the client uses the same service instance.

```
using System;
using System.Globalization;
using System.MessageBus;
using System.MessageBus.Services;

namespace WiseOwl {
  [DialogPortType (Name="Time",
                   Namespace="http://www.wiseowl.com/WebServices")]
  public class Time {
    [ServiceMethod]
    public string GetUtcTimeAndDate(string culture) {
      Console.WriteLine ("Client requested UTC time for culture {0}", culture);
      CultureInfo ci = new CultureInfo (culture);
      return DateTime.UtcNow.ToString ("F", ci);
    }
  }
}
```

The client could pass an object or an interface as a method parameter to this service. The service could subsequently call methods on the client's object or interface implementation to initiate callbacks to the client. Using a dialog produces a stateful, persistent session between the client and the service.

The client application for this dialog-based service is also nearly identical to my original Web service client application. In the following example, the *CreateChannel* call creates a session from the client to the service:

```
using System;
using System.Threading;
using System.MessageBus;
using System.MessageBus.Services;
using www_wiseowl_com.WebServices;  // The imported service namespace

public class Client {

  private static AutoResetEvent doneEvent = new AutoResetEvent (false);
```

```csharp
public static void Main(string[] args) {
  string culture = "en-US";
  if (args.Length > 0) culture = args[0];

  // Load the default service environment, called "main".
  ServiceEnvironment se = null;

  try {
    se = ServiceEnvironment.Load();

    // Retrieve the ServiceManager from the default environment
    ServiceManager sm =
      se[typeof(ServiceManager)] as ServiceManager;
    if (sm == null)
      throw new Exception ("ServiceManager is not available.");

    // Start the service environment.
    se.Open();

    // Create a proxy channel that points to the service to call.
    Uri uri = new Uri("soap.tcp://localhost:46000/TimeService/");

    ITimeChannel channel = (ITimeChannel)
        sm.CreateChannel(typeof(ITimeChannel), uri);

    Console.WriteLine(channel.GetUtcTimeAndDate (culture));

    Console.WriteLine("Press enter to stop this client...");
    Console.ReadLine();

    // Either the client or the service can initiate showdown of the session
    // by calling IDialogPortTypeChannel.DoneSending

    // First, register for the Done event
    channel.Done += new EventHandler (DoneHandler);

    // Now, initiate the shutdown
    channel.DoneSending();

    // Now, wait for the shutdown to complete
    doneEvent.WaitOne ();
  }
  catch (Exception e) {
    Console.WriteLine (e);
  }
  finally {
    if (se != null) se.Close();
  }
}
```

```
static void DoneHandler (object sender, EventArgs e) {
  doneEvent.Set();
 }
}
```

Because I decorated the definition of the service with the *DialogPortType-Attribute*, the Wsdlgen utility produces a different definition of the *ITimeChannel* interface definition. The class that implements the interface must also implement the *IDialogPortTypeChannel* interface, resulting in the client and service using a dialog-based communication channel.

Finally, either the client or the service can initiate an orderly shutdown of the session by calling the *IDialogPortTypeChannel.DoneSending* method. The application must then wait for the Done event before terminating. The previously listed client does this after you press **Enter** to allow the client application to shut down.

Programming Transactions

Indigo allows you to pass a transaction across a communication channel, which lets you coordinate operations performed by multiple services. To users, a transaction is a single event that either happens or doesn't happen. To developers, a transaction allows them to write components that can participate in distributed environments.

The *System.Transactions.Transaction* is the base class representing a single transaction. A transaction is created through a *TransactionManager* instance using the *CreateTransaction* or *UnmarshalTransaction* method. Alternatively, you can also create a transaction by calling the static *System.Transactions.Transaction.Create* method, which creates a new transaction with default values.

A transaction can be committed only by the client application that created the transaction. When a client application wants to allow access to the transaction by multiple threads but also wants to prevent those other threads from committing the transaction, the application can use a clone of the transaction. A cloned transaction has the same capabilities as the original transaction, except for the ability to commit the transaction.

Transaction instances can be constructed using the static method *Create* of the *Transaction* class as follows:

```
tx = Transaction.Create();
```

Alternatively, you can create a new *TransactionManager* instance and have it create a transaction for you, as follows:

```
tm = TransactionManager.Create();

tx = tm.CreateTransaction();
```

There are also alternative creation mechanisms that allow you to supply the description, isolation level, and timeout value of the transaction. To commit or roll back a transaction, you will call the respective *Commit* or *Rollback* methods of the *Transaction* instance.

```
tx.Commit();
tx.Rollback();
```

Applications use outcome notifications to release resources or perform other actions after a transaction commits or aborts. A transaction participant that wants to be notified of the commit-abort decision registers for the *Transaction-Outcome* event.

In the following example, we have implemented an event handler named *OnTransactionCompleted* that is going to handle the *TransactionCompleted* event. We then associate this handler with the event by using the following code:

```
tx.TransactionCompleted +=
        new TransactionCompletedEventHandler (OnTransactionCompleted);
```

After you have committed or rolled back the transaction, the *Transaction-Completed* event will be fired automatically by the system, which triggers the execution of *OnTransactionCompleted*.

This example will demonstrate how to enlist in a Microsoft SQL Server transaction. It first creates a transaction, and then opens a connection to *"pubs"*, which is a SQL server database. The example then marshals the transaction object to make it compatible with *EnterpriseService* transactions, and associates the marshaled transaction with the opened connection. The user then has a chance to commit or roll back the transaction.

A new *SqlConnection* is instantiated and opened, with the connecting string set to the local server and the database set to *"pubs"*.

```
conn = new SqlConnection();
conn.ConnectionString =  @"Server=(local);Trusted_Connection=SSPI;Database=pubs
;Enlist=false;";
conn.Open();
```

To enlist the current transaction as a distributed transaction of the open connection, you will call the *EnlistDistributedTransaction* method of the *Sql-Connection* class. However, because this method only takes an object of the

System.EnterpriseServices.ITransaction type, you will need to marshal the existing transaction for compatibility first. The *Marshal* method is used to perform such functionality.

```
estx = (System.EnterpriseServices.ITransaction)
                tx.Marshal(MarshaledTransactionTypeNamespaceUri.ITransaction
);
conn.EnlistDistributedTransaction (estx);
```

Summary

Indigo is the Longhorn general-purpose messaging framework that you can use to build a wide variety of rich communication-based applications. You can build stateless, Web service applications and clients for such applications. You can build RemoteObject services and their clients. You can establish reliable and durable communications sessions.

Indigo is a great communications framework that you can use to build interesting and powerful collaboration applications.

7

Creating Mobility-Aware Longhorn Applications

Mobility is another major theme of Longhorn. Laptops, notebooks, and Tablet PCs are specific and identifiable hardware form factors that support scenarios distinct from those supported by desktop PCs. Mobile PCs comprise a large and growing segment of the overall PC market. Mobile PCs make up about 30 percent of the worldwide PC market now, and the segment is growing more rapidly than desktops.

In absolute terms, shipments of mobile PCs in the United States and Western Europe have increased year after year, whereas desktop shipments have declined.[1] Given that laptops cost more than desktops and given an economy in which the overall PC market is shrinking, the growth of laptop shipments and share is a striking and important trend.

The Japanese market is even more favorable for mobile PCs. In Japan, laptops account for nearly 50 percent of the PC market.

The latest forecasts from IDC and Gartner Dataquest (March 2003) agree that laptop share will continue to increase through the next several years. By fiscal year 2007, these forecasts show mobile PC share of 30 percent in the United States, 33 percent in Western Europe, and 56 percent in Japan. The forecasts also agree that this trend applies to both the consumer and the enterprise markets.

---

1. *IDC PC Tracker* (June 2002).

Applications should be written with mobility in mind for the following key reasons:

- Mobile PCs are a growing segment of both the enterprise and the consumer PC markets. The rapid expansion of wireless technology will only accelerate this trend.

- Laptops cost more than desktops: They are a premium PC product. The growing number of buyers who are choosing laptops—who pay more despite getting less traditional capability—demonstrates that mobility has real value.

- A significant amount of industry research and development is focused on mobile PCs, so the value associated with applications on these PCs should increase. Innovations in both hardware and software will yield to new and improved mobile PCs with low-power processors, innovative form factors (such as the Tablet PC), longer battery life, and improved performance.

Areas of ongoing investment for Longhorn mobility include the following:

- Anywhere wireless networking (the ability to move between wireless environments)

- Peer-to-peer collaboration

- Hot docking and undocking (easy and stable)

- Multimonitor support for docking and meeting room projection scenarios

- Improved power management (for longer battery life)

- Fast, consistent resume from standby

- Find me, hide me (management of notifications)

- Offline access and seamless synchronization of data

- Location awareness and location-aware services

Some of the fundamentals that software designers need to consider while designing applications for Longhorn mobile scenarios are power management, form factor (including docking/undocking and readability), and network awareness. Each of these fundamentals is discussed in the following sections.

Power Management

The mobility trends described earlier will gradually cause two fundamental shifts in the way most people use their computers. First, people take their PCs with them when they leave their offices to work offsite, to travel, or to attend meetings. Second, people now expect to be able to use their PCs much more like they do PDAs and cell phones, without having to go through long startup and shutdown procedures between sessions.

To meet these expectations, the hardware, operating system, and applications must each do their part to help realize extended battery life and fast, reliable system standby and resume transitions. Through the OnNow power management initiatives, Microsoft has been working since the release of Windows 98 to drive battery life and availability improvements in PC hardware, the core Windows components, and applications.

Longhorn continues this investment with several key new features for improved power management, including a redesigned and enhanced kernel power policy manager. Extensions to the power manager will provide a common framework for applications and devices to register for and receive notifications of important system power events, including the user's current power preferences (for example, the user currently wants maximum battery life or maximum performance), and notifications of when the remaining battery capacity crosses specific thresholds (for example, remaining battery capacity is 30 percent).

An application can also use the power policy manager to handle the storage and retrieval of its application-specific power settings with the current user system power policy. When a power transition occurs that affects a power setting that the application has registered for, the power manager will notify the application with an updated value for the power setting. The power manager can handle all overhead of storing, managing, and retrieving power settings for an application. This can significantly reduce the work required by the application to support intelligent and efficient power-aware behavior.

Coinciding with the release of Windows 98, Microsoft published a white paper on designing power-aware applications: "OnNow Power Management Architecture for Applications." Many of the fundamental design and implementation guidelines in this paper are unchanged under the new Longhorn power manager framework. Before we examine what has changed for Longhorn applications, it's worth reviewing what has not.

First and foremost, applications should respond to and make proper use of the system power broadcast (WM_POWERBROADCAST) messages. When the system is about to go to sleep, Windows will broadcast a sleep query message, along with a flag indicating whether applications are allowed to display the user interface (UI). Regardless of the state of the "UI allowed" flag, applications should make every effort to prepare for sleep without querying or notifying the user. When the flag is set to disallow UI, it usually indicates that the user is unable to see and respond to the UI—for example, when the lid on a laptop is closed. Unless an application is in the middle of an uninterruptible operation, it should use the sleep query message to quickly and silently save its state so that it can seamlessly resume when the system wakes up again. In particular, because network connections and file handles are likely to be invalid after a standby/resume transition, applications should autosave any open files and silently close open file handles as part of their sleep preparation sequence.

Windows monitors system utilization and user input to detect when the system is being actively used, and depending on current power policy settings, it might turn off specific devices or transition the entire system to the standby state (ACPI-defined S3, or suspend to RAM state) to save power after the idle time-out has expired. Longhorn will be *more aggressive* about reducing system power consumption. The S3 system standby sleep state will be used much more frequently than in earlier versions of Windows.

Users often perform tasks with their PCs that might not be detected by the system as actual activity. One common example is when a user is presenting a document to others. Applications designed to understand such a presentation mode can call Windows application programming interfaces (APIs) to tell the power manager that the system or display is currently required, thus preventing the idle timers from expiring.

However, the user might be running an application such as a spreadsheet that has no concept of this presentation scenario and does not use these API calls to prevent system power management events. Windows users frequently complain about the display turning off in this case. To address this problem, Longhorn will include a "keep the system and display on" setting, which will temporarily override current power policy values; this setting will be easily accessible from the system battery meter. When the user chooses this setting, all idle timers will be disabled until the temporary override expires or is explicitly canceled.

Applications can also use timer objects to schedule the system to wake or to ensure that the system will be available at a predetermined time. This enables applications to schedule tasks such as backup, media recording, and the like.

Applications should be aware that the level of activity generated by a task might fall below the system idle detection threshold, and thus the system might transition to a low-power standby state at any time. To prevent this, applications should call the *SetThreadExecutionState* API when performing critical work. This ensures that the system will remain in the working state for the duration of the task. Applications must also take care to call the *SetThreadExecutionState* API again when the work is complete, thus allowing the system to continue to monitor system utilization and transition to a low-power state as indicated by the current power policy.

Application developers should also be aware of how their designs affect processor power management features. Recent mobile CPU designs have achieved impressive power efficiency through the use of processor idle sleep states (ACPI-defined C states) and dynamic voltage and frequency scaling technologies, otherwise known as *performance states*. These technologies dynamically reduce processor power consumption while providing performance on demand. However, periodic activity will cause the processor to exit the low-power idle sleep state (C state), and increases in CPU utilization might cause the operating system to increase the current CPU performance state, resulting in greatly increased CPU power consumption. You should test and profile applications on mobile or desktop systems employing these power-saving technologies to evaluate and minimize the effect the application has on processor power consumption.

Software developers should consider how application features can be scaled back based on the system power state (for example, is the system running on utility or battery power?) and the current power policy (for example, the user has indicated, via selecting a power policy, that she wants maximum battery life). In such cases, the user is agreeing to a reduced experience in exchange for the longest possible battery life. Software features that are good candidates for scaling or temporary suspension when operating the system in low-power modes include the following:

■   Nonessential background content processing such as spelling checking, grammar checking, pagination, and indexing for future searches. Some tasks, such as indexing, can be turned off entirely while the system is running on a battery, others can reduce their processing, and therefore power, requirements by reducing the update frequency.

■   Visual elements and effects such as thumbnail and preview panes, animations, and media playback. Thumbnail and preview pane update frequency should be reduced to less than once per second. Animations and playback can be scaled by reducing size and frame rate. Some effects should be turned off entirely if they are nonessential and cannot scale gracefully.

■ Polling for status changes and new data. Polling is almost always an inferior design, and should be avoided whenever possible. Any polling activity necessary should be scaled down in frequency to less than one activity per second. When possible, polling should be replaced by notifications or synchronous designs.

```
// This program demonstrates how a managed program can notice the
// power state of the machine changing, and respond appropriately:
// changing intervals of regularly performed actions, and suspending
// or resuming actions.

using System;
using System.Threading;
using System.Runtime.InteropServices;
using Microsoft.Win32;

namespace PowerSample {
  class PowerSample {
    private PowerThread[] _threads;

    // this struct and system API call are described in MSDN. It
    // does not take much interop to get a lot of information
    // about the machine.

    enum _ACLineStatus : byte {
      Offline = 0, Online = 1, Unknown = 255
    }
    enum _BatteryFlag : byte {
      High = 1, Low = 2, Critical = 4, Charging = 8,
      NoSystemBattery = 128, Unknown = 255
    }

    internal struct SystemPowerStatus {
      public _ACLineStatus ACLineStatus;
      public _BatteryFlag  BatteryFlag;
      public byte          BatteryLifePercent;
      public byte          Reserved1;
      public uint          BatteryLifeTime;
      public uint          BatteryFullLifeTime;
    }

    [DllImport("kernel32")]
    internal static extern
    bool GetSystemPowerStatus (out SystemPowerStatus sps);
```

```
// these flags and system API call are also described in MSDN.

[Flags]
enum ExecutionState : uint {
  SystemRequired        = 0x01,
  SystemDisplayRequired = 0x02,
  UserPresent           = 0x04,
  Continuous            = 0x80000000,
}


[DllImport("kernel32")] internal static extern
uint SetThreadExecutionState (ExecutionState esFlags);

// This nested class represents application code with periodic
// processing to do. It encapsulates a Thread object. This
// object is responsive to a method to let it know the power
// state of the machine; when the machine goes from AC to DC
// power, we suspend all low priority processing, and increase
// the interval at which we perform other periodic processing.
//
// In the best of all possible worlds, the application
// programmer would not be required to poll in worker threads
// like this; being sensitive to the system's power state
// minimizes the negative consequences of this kind of code.
// This example assumes that there is some periodic activity
// that needs to occur.

class PowerThread {
  private bool _lowPriority;
  private Thread _thread;
  private string _name;

  // storage used primarily in the context of the worker thread
  private int _sleepDelay;
  private bool _onBattery;

  public PowerThread(string name, bool lowPriority) {
    this._name = name;
    this._lowPriority = lowPriority;

    this._thread = null;
    this._sleepDelay = lowPriority ? 5000 : 1000;
    this._onBattery = false;
  }

  public void Start() {
    if (null == this._thread) {
      this._thread = new Thread(new ThreadStart(ThreadProc));
```

```
    this._thread.IsBackground = true;

    if (this._lowPriority) {
      this._thread.Priority = ThreadPriority.Lowest;
    }

    this._thread.Start();

    // When the thread is initialized, we examine the
    // power state of the machine and notify the
    // thread. This way the initial state of the
    // thread (once it's initialized) will be
    // consistent with the power state of the machine.
    SystemPowerStatus status = new SystemPowerStatus();
    if (GetSystemPowerStatus (out status)) {
      this.PowerChange(status);
    }
  }
}

private void ThreadProc() {
  while (true) {
    int milliseconds = _sleepDelay;
    if (this._onBattery) {
      // This is where we artificially slow things
      // down on DC power. Your application might
      // adopt a different strategy for minimizing
      // power use while on DC.
      milliseconds *= 2;
    }
    else {
      // when on AC, we keep the computer awake
      // every time we do some processing. Once
      // we're done with our processing, the
      // computer will go back to the normal timeout
      // as dictated by the kernel power policy.
      SetThreadExecutionState(ES_SYSTEM_REQUIRED);
    }

    Console.WriteLine(_name + " working every "
        + milliseconds.ToString()
        + " milliseconds "
        + (this._onBattery ? "and letting system time out"
                           : "and reserving system")
        );
```

```
        Thread.Sleep(milliseconds);
    }
  }


  public void PowerChange (SystemPowerStatus status) {
    // the significance of the numbers in the
    // SYSTEM_POWER_STATUS fields is described in MSDN
    if (ACLineStatus.Online == status.ACLineStatus &&
        true == _onBattery) {
      // system is now on AC power
      Console.WriteLine(_name + " transitioning to AC power");
      _onBattery = false;

      if (true == this._lowPriority) {
        Console.WriteLine("Resuming " + this._name);
        this._thread.Resume();
      }
    }
    else if (0 == status.ACLineStatus && false == _onBattery) {
      // AC is offline (we've gone on DC - battery or UPS)
      Console.WriteLine(_name + " transitioning to DC power");
      _onBattery = true;

      if (true == this._lowPriority) {
        Console.WriteLine ("Suspending " + this._name);
        this._thread.Suspend();
      }
    }
  }
}


// This is our event handler for the system event. The event
// indicates whether the power state of the machine has
// changed, or if we've come back from a standby, etc. Our
// behavior is the same in any case - we're just going to turn
// around and get more detailed information about the power
// state of the machine, and feed that information to our
// worker threads.
void OnPowerModeChange(object obj, PowerModeChangedEventArgs e) {
  if (e.Mode == PowerModes.StatusChange) {
    Console.WriteLine("Power status or capacity change detected");
    if (null != this._threads) {
      SystemPowerStatus status = new SystemPowerStatus();

      if (GetSystemPowerStatus (out status)) {
        foreach (PowerThread victim in this._threads) {
          victim.PowerChange(status);
        }
```

```
        }
      }
    }
  }

  // This routine sets up an event hook, creates a few worker
  // threads, lets the threads run for a while (being responsive
  // to power changes), and then terminates.
  void Go () {
    SystemEvents.PowerModeChanged +=
            new PowerModeChangedEventHandler(OnPowerModeChange);

    Console.WriteLine("Creating worker threads");

    this._threads = new PowerThread[3];
    this._threads[0] = new PowerThread("Worker thread 1", false);
    this._threads[1] = new PowerThread("Worker thread 2", false);
    this._threads[2] = new PowerThread("Low-priority thread", true);

    foreach (PowerThread victim in this._threads) {
      victim.Start();
    }

    Console.WriteLine ("Working for five minutes");
    Console.WriteLine ("(Please trip over the power cord now!)");
    Thread.Sleep(5 * 60 * 1000);

    Console.WriteLine("Ending worker threads - bye");
  }

  static void Main (string[] args) {
    PowerSample ps = new PowerSample();

    if (null != ps) ps.Go ();
  }
}
```

Form Factor

Laptops, notebooks, and Tablet PCs present challenges to application developers not encountered on desktop PCs. These challenges include grab-and-go docking and readability.

Grab-and-Go Docking

One feature of Longhorn laptops and Tablet PCs is the ability to remove the computer from a docking station or port at any time, without prior warning. Grab-and-go docking presents a challenge for the software designer, who must consider computer connectivity to mass storage devices (hard disks in docking stations, CD-R drives, 1394 hard disks, and others). Any device to which the user is currently writing data or from which the user is reading data can suddenly be disconnected. Software developers should design fallbacks for all these actions—preferably fallbacks that do not require user interaction and are self-healing when device connectivity is restored.

Many Longhorn mobile PC form factors will include two display adapters: one for the built-in screen and one for an external monitor that is used while the device is docked. Consider how your application works when a user interacts with it by using a pen on a Tablet PC or runs another application on an external monitor. You can take advantage of both displays simultaneously. While docked, the built-in display becomes a private display that interacts with the pen, while the external screen is the public interface.

Data such as files, contacts, and devices should be synchronized using the Longhorn Synchronization Manager. The Synchronization Manager will provide users with a single place to synchronize all data.

Designing for Readability

Reading is a common and frequent task for mobile PC users. You can take advantage of mobile PCs as a reading tool by ensuring that your application provides the following capabilities:

- Responds to page-up and page-down events.

- Uses smooth scrolling (real time, no flashing) to allow a user's eye to track the movement of a document as the user scrolls.

- Provides a riffle control that uses a half-second transition per move and per repeat. A riffle control enables users to flip through pages or screens of content quickly.

- Provides a rich contrast between the background and the content of the document so that it is readable even when viewed from an angle or when some glare exists.

- Uses colors with a rich contrast for better readability. Do not use yellows, oranges, or other light colors for important items on the screen. Dark colors are easier to distinguish on backlit screens.

Network Awareness

In the past, network-connected machines were stationary devices permanently connected to a network. Applications were developed with this assumption in mind. In the new world of wireless access and mobile devices, application developers can no longer assume that the network is always present or that there is only a single path to a resource. Even though the Transmission Control Protocol (TCP) has complex algorithms to ensure guaranteed delivery, it cannot overcome the transient nature of the mobile user's network environment. Both wireless networking and grab-and-go docking mean that network connections and external hard disks can become disconnected without warning. Although this has always been a concern of desktop applications, these potential problems become much more common on mobile PCs. Applications should be able to handle these dynamic and divergent network environments.

Although each application has its own unique constraints on network behavior, developers should consider implementing several features:

- **Implicit online/offline switching**   If your application has two separate modes for online and offline behavior, take advantage of the network presence detection in Longhorn and switch between them automatically, without requiring user action or approval.

- **Background and cached file writing**   Rather than locking the UI when writing to a file, save immediately to a known local file, and attempt to update the real file in the background.

- **Delayed file writing**   Add functional dexterity by allowing users to save and close a file without the storage available. Prompt users for actions only when necessary (for example, if the online and offline versions become unsynchronized).

- **Cache copies of embedded or linked data**   For example, at a minimum, keep a static representation of all objects in your file as bitmaps. That way, if the source disappears, users can at least perform basic rendering.

You should continue to design your software to account for sudden disconnection from network resources, including the capability to automatically or manually store data on a local device, and use time-outs on all network actions. Some considerations in this regard include the following:

- Handling sudden removal and addition of network connections and peripherals.

■ Implementing operations that can recover if problems arise, such as load or save operations to a USB, 1394 hard disk, or CD peripheral. Then, when such operations are interrupted with a docking or undocking action, they can be restarted later.

■ Using best practices for network connectivity. Your application should operate seamlessly in situations where networks are temporarily unavailable or set or reset themselves. For example, your application should include the following capabilities:

❑ Handle connectivity transitions.

❑ Provide auto reconnection that does not require restarting the application.

❑ Give clear feedback of network availability so that the user is aware of this state.

❑ Have the ability to be used offline. It is not unusual for a wireless network connection to be intermittent or for users to be offline for a short time without realizing it. Your application should behave seamlessly in these situations. The application should not stop responding while the network is unavailable.

❑ Implement automatic synchronization capability when a connection is reestablished, if your application needs to synchronize offline and online data. It is tedious for users to have to remember the explicit steps for synchronizing. Manual synchronization is unnecessary if your application can detect a reconnection to the network and can run automatic data synchronization.

You can choose from many methods to make both streaming and transactions applications perform quickly and effectively across transient and low bandwidth networks. MSDN provides several white papers that deal exclusively with that subject. Briefly, these white papers conclude that a well-written network application should provide the following features:

■ Limit the number of small transactions. Roundtrips between server and host are expensive.

■ Be tested with the applications in environments that have packet loss and low bandwidth.

■ Have intelligent error handling systems, which keep the user informed.

■ Treat the network as an unreliable resource.

You need to keep in mind several other situations that apply to a mobile user:

■ The disappearance of the network completely

■ Changes in the network properties

■ What happens when a mobile user moves to a new valid network that does not have the resources the application needs

■ Dramatic changes in bandwidth

Several improvements in Longhorn will make it simpler to address some of these issues. Network Location API (NLA) will provide a single place where an application can get all the network parameters for a machine. The API will also inform the application whether the parameters have been changed and will even give the application some network context information.

For each interface, the API will provide IP address and configuration information, domain name, adapter GUIDs, and context information. NLA will assign the connection to one of the categories described in the following table.

Type	Definition
Ad hoc	The interface is on an ad hoc network not connected to any other network.
Managed	The interface is connected to a managed "secure" network such as an enterprise, with a Windows domain controller.
Unmanaged	The interface is not connected to a Windows domain.
Unknown	The service is unable to determine the connection's characteristics.

Each of these categories, with the exception of ad hoc, can also indicate the Internet flag, as described in the following table.

Flag	Definition
Internet	The interface has Internet connectivity, defined as being able to resolve a common DNS A record from the Internet.

Although these categories are not foolproof, they give the application a good idea of where the host is on the network.

Although NLA helps with traversing the network, it does not solve the problem of the absence of a network resource on a valid network. In this case, the application can wait for the send failure, but this provides little real information about why the failure happened. A more elegant and effective solution is an *application layer ping*.

A standard Internet Control Message Protocol (ICMP) echo of the resource's name provides the application with little information. The ICMP response can fail for many reasons other than the absence of the resource. Broken name resolution and blocking of ICMP responses (common for security reasons) could easily provide false negatives. An application ping or probe can provide much more information than just the presence of the resource on the new network. It tells the application not only that the server is responding but also whether the application on the server is responsive.

You can also use an application ping to calculate the throughput of a connection, which is extremely useful when the user is moving from a high-bandwidth wired connection to a low-bandwidth wide area network (WAN) connection.

Here is a formula that can assist with calculating the true capacity of the connection:

$$(\textbf{OID\_GEN\_LINK\_SPEED}*RTT(secs)) = capacity\ (bps)$$

After the application has knowledge of the throughput of the connection, it can make intelligent decisions about what type of transactions are appropriate for the size of the pipe. For example, an application can use this information to determine whether the download of a large piece of data would be unreasonable given the network conditions. Applications can tailor their behavior to the conditions.

In the near-term, wireless WAN will be severely bandwidth restricted. The quoted maximum speeds are possible only under optimal conditions. The user would need to be stationary, and with most technologies, only one user per cell could get the full amount of bandwidth allowed by the topology. Unfortunately, these technologies also introduce highly varied amounts of delay. A user could easily see roundtrip time changes from 500 ms to 3000 ms from packet to packet. This discrepancy can make a single ping or probe provide erroneous information to the application about current conditions. This problem can be countered by calculating averages gathered over the history of the connection.

Summary

With increased laptop, notebook, and Tablet PC sales, Microsoft recognizes the value of improving mobile PC use. Longhorn will emphasize a number of mobility scenarios that application developers should be aware of as they design Longhorn-compatible software. Keeping in mind power management, docking/undocking (including data synchronization), and network awareness will be key in building and deploying Longhorn applications for mobile PCs.

Index

Brent Rector

Brent Rector is president and founder of Wise Owl Consulting (*www.wiseowl.com*), and has over three decades of experience in software development. Brent has designed and implemented operating systems as well as new computer programming languages and their compilers. Brent started developing Windows applications using Windows 1*x* beta in 1985 and has been involved in Windows development ever since. He is the author and coauthor of numerous Windows programming books, including *ATL Internals* and *Win32 Programming*. Brent is also the author of Demeanor for .NET—the premier code obfuscator for .NET applications.